A Guide to Electronic Music and Synthesizers

by Walter Sear.

Omnibus Press

Omnibus Press Ltd.,
A division of Book Sales Ltd.,
78, Newman Street,
London W1P 3LA, England.

Book Sales Pty Ltd.,
27, Clarendon Street,
Artarmon, Sydney, 2064,
Australia

Printed in Great Britain by
The Camelot Press Ltd, Southampton

ISBN 0.86001.210.7
AM1405C

Contents

Preface   5

1. Sound   7

2. The Electronic Generation of Sound   24

3. The Recording of Sound   40

4. Some Classical Tape Recorder Electronic Music   53
    Techniques

5. The Electronic Music Synthesizer   55

6. Using Electronic Music Synthesizers to Create Music   61

7. Voltage Control Sources   72

8. Additional Synthesizer Accessories   81

9. Interconnecting Various Synthesizer Components   85

10. Salient Features of Various Synthesizers   88

Conclusion   90

Preface

Electronic music has become an important part of our musical culture. Motion picture background scores, television programs and commercials, "pop" music and serious works performed in the concert hall have all come to use these new electronic devices as an integral part of sound and music-making equipment. A new family of musical instruments has come into its own as an expressive and versatile ensemble.

In the discussion which follows, the term "electronic music" does not represent an aesthetic concept any more than "stringed instrument" would be used to connote an aesthetic concept. We refer only to a family of instruments which generate and treat sounds through electronic means. How the composer makes music out of these sounds is an aesthetic problem no different from the problem of making music with conventional instruments, except that electronic instruments provide far greater tonal range; therefore aesthetic judgment becomes far more critical. If we seat a gorilla at a fine concert grand piano and the musical results are bad, we obviously should blame the gorilla and not the piano.

It is the intent of the author to describe the basic ideas, and to explain the basic vocabulary needed for an elementary understanding of sound, acoustics, basic electricity and magnetism necessary to the understanding of electronic music. In fact, since the nonelectronic musician is so intimately involved today with recording, and has always had to understand acoustics, it becomes essential for all musicians to have this knowledge.

Because we have to deal with some rather technical ideas and concepts, it has been necessary at times to oversimplify certain terms rather than become involved with a great deal of text and mathematics. Should the student wish a more technical and scientific description, these are readily available in more specialized texts.

In the chapters on the synthesizer proper, we have described basic concepts and functions rather than "how to do," feeling that if each element of the generation, treatment and amplification of sound is understood, a much wider range of musical thought will result. We have not described specific set-ups for producing specific sounds, since these combinations on the synthesizer are almost numberless.

It is the hope of the author that this book will establish a foundation of interest, and that students will go on to produce a truly new and meaningful music that will communicate human ideas and human emotions to others.

New York City   W.S.
June 1972

1. Sound

Introduction

Until the early twentieth century all musical sounds, excluding the human voice, were produced by mechanical means. These "acoustical" instruments are divided into four basic families:

1. String, where a stretched string is set into motion either by drawing a bow across it or by plucking it;

2. Brass, where air forced through taut lips sets a confined air column into vibration;

3. Woodwind, where air is blown against a metal or woodlike reed, setting a confined air column into vibration; and

4. Percussion, where metal, wood, hide or fiber material is set into vibration by being struck with the hand or some form of mallet.

In most cases conventional instruments use some form of a resonator to amplify the sound produced.

In the case of electronic instruments, the sound source, rather than being struck, blown, plucked or bowed, consists of an electrical circuit which generates an oscillating electrical current. This current, in turn, is amplified electronically, then converted into sound waves through the medium of a loudspeaker. Since the loudspeaker is a device for converting one form of energy (electricity) into another (sound energy), we call this device a *transducer.*

Throughout the history of music and musical instruments, musicians and instrument makers have always designed new and improved instruments as new types of materials and technologies became available. If we trace the development of any of our modern instruments, we can see how scientists and technicians have contributed to their advancement. This is an ongoing process, and we find many modern materials being used on rather old acoustical instruments. Parts made of modern plastics, such as Delrin and Teflon, for instance, are almost standard in modern pianos and harpsichords. Drawn steel wire is definitely standard on such traditional instruments as the violin.

It was only natural, then, that as the electronic technology was developed, musicians began to experiment with its application to the production of sound. Another element, which came about only recently, is that, as our concert halls have become larger and larger, the acoustical resonators and mechanical tone generators were not capable of producing sounds of sufficient loudness to be heard adequately. Therefore many modern concert halls use electronic devices to amplify acoustical instruments.

The electronic musical family has also come to include hybrid instruments with a mechanical sound-producing element amplified by electronic rather than acoustical means. The electric guitar is probably the most common of these.

Let us look into the nature of sound and its treatment by electronic means.

A. The Physics of Sound

For sound to exist, three things are necessary: *generation, transmission* and *perception*.

Sound is generated when an object is set to *vibrating*. Vibration is an *oscillatory motion* (back and forth at regular intervals, like a pendulum) of a string, reed, loudspeaker, etc. Transmission occurs when the vibrating object sets up pressure waves as it moves toward the receiver, and rarefaction waves (a slight vacuum) as it moves away. Usually, the transmitting medium is air, but sound can be transmitted by a transfer of energy from the vibrating object to anything else that can be set into *sympathetic motion*. If there is no transmitting medium, there is no sound. A loudspeaker on the moon, where there is no atmosphere to transmit the sound, cannot be heard even a few inches away. The denser the transmitting medium, i.e. the closer together the molecules are (as in water, for example), the faster the sound will move through it.

For the purpose of our discussion, let us assume that sound is being transmitted through the air. The slight pressures and vacuums that are created in the air by the vibrating object are called *wave compressions* and *wave rarefactions*. As the vibrating object moves in one direction, it bumps into a particle of air, which in turn bumps into the next particle of air, and so on until the energy is dissipated. Due to the elasticity of the vibrating object, it now pulls back from its extension and causes a slight vacuum, which draws a particle of air back. This, in turn, draws the next particle of air back, and so on until the energy is dissipated.

This back-and-forth round trip is called a *cycle*, and the number of times the cycle recurs within the space of a second is the *frequency*. The fewer cycles there are per second, the lower will be the pitch of the resulting sound. Logically, then, the more cycles per second, the higher the pitch. In tribute to the famous German physicist, Heinrich Rudolph Hertz (1857-94), his last name, abbreviated to "Hz.," is used in place of the phrase "cycles per second." *Audible sound,* i.e. the range of frequencies which human ears are normally capable of perceiving, is between 20 and 15,000 Hz. Below 20 to 25 Hz. we tend to hear only so many separate pops. Above 15,000 Hz. most of us hear little, unless the sound is very loud.

If we strike a gong gently, it will sound soft. If we hit it harder, the sound is louder. The reason for this is that more air is set into motion in proportion to the amount of energy used to generate the sound. The greater the force that sets an object into its vibrating motion (the harder you hit the gong), the greater will be the vibration, i.e. the farther away the object will move from where it was resting before being made to vibrate. The extent of this movement determines the degree of compressions and rarefactions in the air. We call this *amplitude,* or loudness.

Each particle of air is set into oscillatory motion, back and forth. It does not move in only one direction, as a current of air does. We call this *wave motion* or *propagation.* For example, let us visualize a pond on a very calm day. The surface of the water is glassy smooth. If we throw a small stone near the center of the pond, a series of concentric waves is generated at regular intervals away from where the stone struck the water. Reason: as the stone strikes the water, it pushes the water away at the point of contact. As the stone pierces the surface of the water, a *positive wave* on the surface of the pond is formed. As the stone passes below the surface of the pond, it sucks water in behind it, forming an indentation below the surface which we call a *trough,* or *negative wave.*

Meanwhile, the particles of water in the positive wave has transmitted their energy to adjacent particles, and a series of concentric waves and troughs are formed in ever-widening circles away from the point of surface contact with the stone. If a leaf is floating on the surface of the pond, the waves will not push it toward the shore; rather, the leaf will bob up and down, showing that the water is not moving like a current, but that the particles of water are bumping into each other and transmitting the wave energy. If we observe closely, we will also notice that each crest (positive wave) and each trough (negative wave) becomes less and less high and deep as it moves away from the energy source, which in this case is the stone (Figure 1).

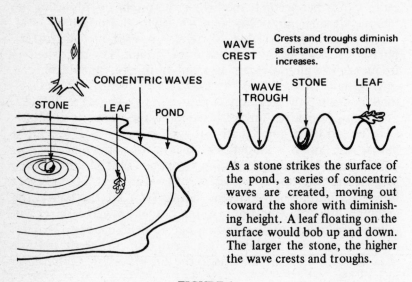

As a stone strikes the surface of the pond, a series of concentric waves are created, moving out toward the shore with diminishing height. A leaf floating on the surface would bob up and down. The larger the stone, the higher the wave crests and troughs.

FIGURE 1

We can measure this decrease in intensity of the waves as they move away from the energy source and find that all has been done in accordance with a law which generally applies to sound energy as well as most other forms of energy, such as light, radio waves, heat, etc. This law is called the *reciprocal of the square of the distance (inverse square law)*. It means that, as we move away from an energy source, the energy level tends to dissipate according to a set mathematical formula. We all know that the farther away from a light bulb we get, the dimmer the light becomes; likewise, the farther we get from a loudspeaker, the softer the sound becomes. This is important to keep in mind when explaining the dissipation of sound as it radiates away from its source.

Now, let us go back to the pond. The surface has resumed its calmness, but this time we are not going to throw a stone into the pond. Let's throw a large rock into the pond. We will see that the wave crests (positive) and wave troughs (negative) will be much larger than before. The floating leaf will bob up and down much farther, while still retaining the same basic position on the surface in relation to where the rock struck the surface. We could say, then, that the waves were generated with greater amplitude than before.

In our first example the waves diminished as they moved toward the shore of the pond in the ratio of the reciprocal of the square of the distance law, and when they reached the shore, there was very little disturbance of the shoreline itself. When we threw the large rock into the pond, the resulting higher waves might still have enough energy upon reaching the shore to erode some of the shoreline away. Too great an amplitude of sound wave energy can have the same effect on a delicate microphone or on our ears.

We can formulate a description of sound now by saying that it is a series of oscillating movements of an object which causes corresponding periodic compressions and rarefactions in the air between the frequencies of 20 and 15,000 Hz.

This would look like a long coilspring or a 'Slinky' toy (Figure 2). It can be perceived (heard) only by our ears if the

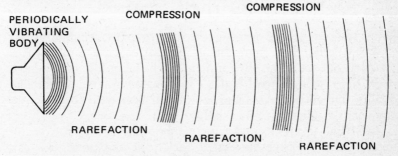

PERIODICALLY VIBRATING BODY

COMPRESSION

COMPRESSION

RAREFACTION

RAREFACTION

RAREFACTION

Sound can be described as a periodic series of oscillating movements of an object which causes corresponding periodic compressions and rarefactions in the air.

A long coil spring like a 'Slinky' toy can be used to visualize sound transmission in air.

FIGURE 2

amplitude (loudness) is within the dynamic range of our hearing. If the sound is too soft to be heard, we say that the sound is below our *threshold of hearing* (which varies from person to person). As the amplitude increases we will eventually reach what is called the *threshold of pain*. As you can imagine, it is at this point that you will intuitively cover your ears with your hands. The intensity of sound can be not only painful, but can cause loss of hearing. (A form of Chinese torture used to be to tie the victim directly under a large bell. The bell was struck over and over until the victim lost his hearing and eventually died from the effects of high energy [amplitude] sound waves. Sometimes we have to live in a high-noise environment; although it takes a little longer than the Chinese torture, the results are remarkably similar. Noise has become one of the more serious environmental threats.)

We use a unit of measurement for the loudness of sound called a *decibel,* which is one tenth of a *bel.* A bel, named after Alexander Graham Bell (1847-1922), is the unit of an exponential scale of sound pressure measurement, and the decibel is abbreviated as *db.* It is the standard unit for measuring the loudness of a sound.

B. The Perception of Sound

Since we hear sound in a specific environment, it is important to know how that environment will affect the sound waves reaching our ears. The environment might be outdoors in a large open field, in a concert hall, or in your own living room. The quality and character of the sound will vary with the environment. Let's go back to the pond.

This time let us assume that the shoreline is very rocky and hard. After we have thrown a rock into the pond, we can observe the waves radiating out toward the shore from where the rock entered the water. As the waves reach the shore, we can see that upon hitting the hard shoreline, some of the wave motion is reflected back toward the center of the pond. These reflected waves will be of much less amplitude (height), but they will be of the same frequency. In the case of sound waves, it is called *echo,* and it can be described as the reflection of sound waves from a hard surface. We have all had experience with echoes. In fact, experts can tell blindfolded the general size of a room simply by its echoing characteristics (Figure 3).

Back at the pond, we can easily notice that the farther from the shore the spot is where the rock hit the surface, the longer it will take for the waves to reach the shoreline and be reflected back to the point of generation. With sound waves the same holds true. The greater the distance the reflecting surface is from the sound source, the longer it will take for the echo to return. Since the law of the reciprocal of the square of the distance applies, we can say that the greater the distance the sound has to travel, the softer it will be on its return from the

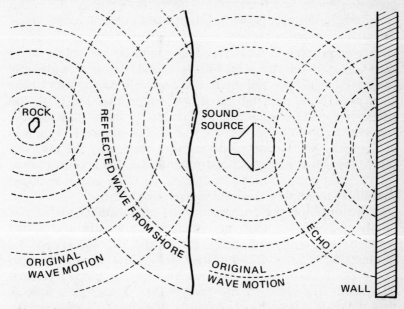

Upon hitting a hard surface, wave motion is reflected toward the original source.

FIGURE 3

reflecting surface. All sound frequencies travel at the same speed—approximately 1,100 feet per second. We say approximately 1,100 feet, because the density, humidity and temperature of the air will alter this slightly. Knowing this figure, we can determine how far away a reflecting surface is from us. If we happen to be on a mountain side, for instance, and want to know the distance to the next peak, we can shout and time the echo return. If it takes six seconds for the echo to return, we can calculate that the other peak is three seconds away from us (three seconds for our voice to get to the peak and three seconds for it to return), and so we know we are about 3,300 feet away. A noise source such as lightning can tell us how far away a thunderstorm may be. If we see a flash of lightning, which we see instantaneously, and then hear the thunder five seconds later, we know that the storm is 5,500 feet away from us.

At the pond, we notice that certain sizes of rocks thrown into the pond will produce a certain frequency of waves. Sometimes, when these waves reach the shoreline, they are reflected in such a way that they crest at the same instant as the incoming waves and therefore reinforce their energy. When this synchronization occurs, we say that the waves are in *resonance*. There is a natural resonance to any confined body of air, which is very important in understanding sound. If we take a water glass and tap on the side with a spoon, we hear a definite frequency, which we call pitch. If we now fill one quarter of the glass with water and tap on it, we notice that the pitch has gotten higher. This is because there is less air in the glass and the *resonant frequency* has become higher. The more water there is in the glass, the less air, and therefore the higher the resonant frequency. Most acoustical instruments use this type of resonator (a given volume of air contained within a nearly enclosed container) to amplify the sound-generating source.

If we examine the construction of any member of the viol family, we can see that, in effect, the resonator is a sealed wooden box with two holes cut in the top for sound. As frequencies become lower, larger resonators are required to reinforce them; it is for this reason that the highest pitched instrument, the violin, is also the smallest. Therefore it follows that the viola is larger than the violin, the cello is larger than the viola, and the double bass is larger than the cello. In the brass family of instruments the air is confined within a brass tube which acts as a resonator. The more air that is confined in a tube, the lower the frequency that the instrument will produce. The woodwind family confines the air within a wooden tube, and the same rule holds true. Sometimes we call these resonators *Helmholtz resonators*, after Hermann Ludwig Ferdinand von Helmholtz (1821-94), the physicist who first described the behavior of resonance and acoustics in detail.

Back to the pond. We have been assuming that the shoreline has been of a hard material; but suppose it is of soft mud and is clogged with plants and weeds. Now the waves will be reflected back in a variety of different directions, all random, and the reflected wave energy will be dissipated so that very little of it will be reflected. We can see that the echo (reflected wave) has been damped, or *attenuated*. Sound waves behave in the same way. Sometimes we want to eliminate or reduce echo. This can be done by eliminating hard reflective surfaces. A soft, rough-surfaced material will attenuate echo. Many materials are made specifically to eliminate or reduce sound reflection.

Acoustical tile, for example, is made of pressed and dried plant stalks. It is soft, with an irregular surface, which tends to dissipate the sound energy by reflecting it in completely random directions. The tile is often used where noise levels have to be reduced, such as in restaurants, recording studios and concert halls, or whenever a room is too "live." This means that there is too much echo and direct reflection of sound (Figure 4).

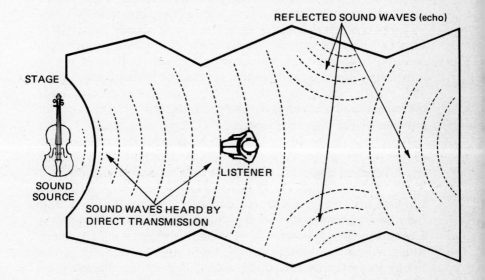

The listener will hear sound both directly from the sound source as well as the echo reflected back from the walls. The time difference between direct transmission and echo will be determined by the distance that the echo has to travel before it is heard by the listener.

FIGURE 4

The degree of liveness (echo) is also determined by the angle at which the sound waves strike a reflecting surface. In the concert hall, where some liveness is needed, there may be a series of nonparallel reflecting walls and surfaces, in which case the sound will be reflected at an angle to another reflecting surface, thus lengthening the time it will take for the sound to return to the stage.

The ear is quite sensitive to these slight differences in timing between the initial sound, which reaches the ear directly, and the much weaker echo.

The ears are so placed on the head that the brain can determine which ear has heard a sound first. Although there are only a few microseconds of delay because of the distance between the ears, the brain can sense this difference and determine from which direction the sound is coming. If someone calls to us in a darkened room, we can easily tell from which direction the voice is coming, and we will intuitively turn toward the source of the sound. When we face the sound source directly, the sound reaches both ears at the same time. Because of echo characteristics, we face the sound source rather than turn 180 degrees with our backs to it. This would also set up a condition wherein the sound would reach both ears simultaneously. Since the brain is able to measure differences in milli- and microseconds, as well as determine differences in level between sound and echo, we can chalk this up to another of the miracles of the Older Engineer.

A large number of echoes can be generated from a single sound source, all arriving at our ears at different intervals, and from different angles, if there are many reflective surfaces in a room. This is called *reverberation*. Often, also, the reflecting surfaces may be set into *sympathetic vibration* and will add their own characteristics to the sound. Sympathetic vibration is a vibration set up as a result of sound waves striking an object which is free to vibrate; the object will vibrate as a result of the energy imparted by the sound waves. This can be illustrated by striking a single note on a piano. If we touch the strings one octave above the note, we will not feel any vibration. However, if we depress the loud pedal, which raises the dampers away from the strings, we can feel the strings one octave above the note struck go into vibration. Sympathetic vibration is a very important part of *acoustics,* which is that branch of the science of physics that deals with sound.

We can perform a number of interesting experiments with the use of a blindfold. Blind people rely on their hearing for a great deal of information, and the blindfold helps us to simulate an environment which forces us to listen more acutely. By clapping our hands sharply we can estimate whether we are indoors or outdoors. We can also estimate the size of the room by the echo, as well as by the liveness, by how loud the echo is in comparison to the intial sound. If you are in a room with a piano, press the loud pedal and listen to the amount of sympathetic vibrations that the piano strings will set up as you clap your hands. This is reverberation from piano strings that are in sympathetic vibration. The quality of sound that you hear, therefore, is strongly influenced by the environment in which it is produced. Now, as a final experiment, with a blindfold on or your eyes shut, just listen to the amount of noise that exists in the room. This background noise is called *ambient,* or *room, noise.* It is so much a part of our natural environment that when we are making a motion picture of a room in which there is a conversation taking place, we have to add room noise in order to make the scene realistic, because the conversation itself is actually recorded in a soundproof studio with a very low, and therefore unnatural, ambient noise level. In the modern world it is this high level of ambient noise that is eroding our hearing as well as our nervous system.

If we were to hear all frequencies of audible sound, from 20 to 15,000 Hz. simultaneously and at random amplitude, we would hear an unpitched hiss which we call *white noise.* Many percussion instruments tend to produce a limited range of this white noise spectrum. However, if the sound frequency is regular and periodic, with a very specific frequency, we call it *pitched sound.*

The note "A" that we tune to in the orchestra has been established by international agreement at 440 Hz. This means a vibration causing 440 compressions and rarefactions per second in the air. What we call an *octave* above this "A" is exactly double the frequency, or 880 Hz. An octave above the 880 Hz. tone is double again, or 1,760 Hz. From this we may observe that the ratio of frequencies between the octave and our original "A" is 2:1. Frequency ratios of the other intervals in our western music scale tend to be in the ratio of small whole numbers. For instance, the perfect fifth is in the ratio of 3:2, the perfect fourth, 4:3, and so on.

The composer must determine aesthetically which pitch relationship he wants, vertically (that is, sounding simultaneously, or *chordal*) and horizontally (linearly, or *melodic*), as well as which unpitched sounds he wants. These elements must then be organized in a time period so as to produce what will seem logical and acceptable to the human ear and mind, or what we may call a meaningful musical experience. Whether he uses natural sounds, conventional instruments, or electronic instruments, the aesthetic problems and solutions are still determined by the human element, filtered through both the composer's and listener's cultural experience. Therefore, both the composer and the listener must apply some effort and experience if the musical presentation is to be truly meaningful.

C. The Elements of Sound

Sound, in its simplest form, may be described as consisting of three functions. The first is the *pitch function;* the second is the *color,* or *timbre, function;* and the third is the *amplitude,* or *loudness, function.* Let us examine them in detail:

1. The *pitch function* has to do with whether there is a predominant frequency or not, and if there is one, what it is, either by letternote name or by frequency in Hz. The higher the frequency, the higher the pitch; the lower the frequency, the lower the pitch. If there is no clearly defined frequency, it becomes noise. A piccolo produces a high-pitched note with definite frequency. A piece of chalk squeaking against a blackboard makes a high-pitched noise since it produces a variety of high frequencies, none of which can be singled out as a predominant pitched note. A tuba produces a low-frequency tone with a definite pitch. The roar of a subway is a low-pitched noise with indeterminate pitch frequency. In between are other tones and noises which could be generally classified as mid-range. *Noise,* then, could be defined as a combination of frequencies comprising so many different pitches that no single pitch is predominant. There is no clear line between pitched and unpitched sound. For example, a bass drum sounds unpitched, yet a bass drummer will tune his instrument to a general pitch area. We must also mention that pitch and noise have in common the additional dimension of *duration,* i.e, the period of time within which they exist. During this period, pitch may move from one definite note to another. This is known as *discrete movement.* Or it may glide through all of the intermediate frequencies between notes, like a smear on the trombone. The musical term for this is a *glissando.* Likewise, noise can move discretely or it can glide from one area to another.

2. The function of *color,* or *timbre,* means the quality and character of a sound. This depends on the number of sounds being generated at the same time and how they interact. A flute

can sound the pitch "A" (440 Hz.), and an oboe can sound the same pitch, yet there is clearly a difference in timbre, which makes it easy to tell one instrument from another. This is due to the specific construction of each instrument, which in turn results in the presence of *overtones*—about which we will have more to say later. Furthermore, some instruments may even change tone color during the playing of a single sustained note. In fact, many instruments are characterized by their change in timbre on each note played. The sitar, because of its sympathetically resonating strings, is a good example of this.

3. The function called *amplitude* is a pattern of loudness within a given period of time. How loudly a sound starts, continues and dies away is important to the consideration of sound. We divide this into three areas. The first is called the *attack period*. On some instruments this is fixed and cannot be altered, as in the case of most percussion instruments and plucked string instruments. Once a sound is started, it can never get louder than the initial attack. The piano is a good example of this. Once the hammer strikes the string and sets it into vibration, the loudness level can only decrease from that point on. The middle portion of the amplitude is called the *sustain period*. On many instruments this is infinitely controllable, depending on the musician. Wind players, for instance, can vary the loudness at will. The final portion of amplitude is called the *decay period,* wherein a sound can be cut off abruptly or die out slowly. These three functions of amplitude may be described collectively as the *envelope* of sound. The envelope is as much the character of certain instruments as is the timbre. If we were to record single notes of a piano or timpani on a tape recorder and then play the tape in reverse, we would find it hard to identify the instruments.

D. Overtones

Generally speaking, acoustical instruments do not produce a single pure tone. While we tend to hear the *fundamental frequency* as the most predominant element, the instrument is actually producing a whole series of higher, and usually closely related, pitches. The ear tends to combine these into a single sound, but with varying color.

If we take a stretched string and set it into vibration by plucking or bowing it, we see that the string is vibrating as a whole between the two confining points. It will produce a given pitch which is determined by the length of the string (the longer it is, the lower the pitch that it will produce), the tension on the string (tuning pins are used to increase or decrease the tension and therefore the pitch), and the mass (weight) of the material of which the string is made. The greater the mass, the lower the pitch, and if we observe, we will see that the double bass has much thicker strings than the violin. As a matter of fact, even the higher strings on the violin are thinner than the lower ones.

If we divide the string exactly in half by gently touching the string at its mid-point, we find the string produces a tone an octave higher than the pitch to which the string was originally tuned; this new tone is an *overtone*. The point at which we touch the string is called a *node,* and the octave produced is called the *first overtone*. As we touch the string in other places, gently sliding our fingers from the mid-point of the string toward one end, certain other pitches are produced. At one-third the distance from either end of the string, we find that another nodal point is reached, and the string will vibrate freely, producing a note an octave and a fifth higher than the fundamental. This is called the *second overtone*. If we continue to move along the string, at a point one-fourth from the end of the string, we find a nodal point that produces a pitch two octaves above the fundamental. This is called the *third overtone*. Continuing, we find that the next nodal point is one-fifth the length of the string and produces a tone two octaves plus a major third above the fundamental. At one-sixth the distance, two octaves and a perfect fifth, at one-seventh the distance, two octaves and a dominant seventh, at one-eighth the distance, a triple octave. By continuing to subdivide, we would eventually find that all of the notes of the chromatic scale could be derived from one string. In actuality, the vibrating string is subdividing by itself many times over, generating many of the harmonics in the *overtone series*. Usually the amplitude of the harmonics is far less than the fundamental pitch. However, the degree of presence of these harmonics determines the timbre of the sound (Figure 5).

As in the case of the vibrating string, a vibrating air column, as found in the brass and woodwind instruments, behaves in the same way. The compressions and rarefactions produce harmonics of varying strengths which produce the particular sound color of that particular instrument. All instruments make use of the overtone series. A bugle player, by changing the tension of his lips, can set the air column into vibration at the fundamental (rarely used), and then play first, second, third, fourth, fifth, and sixth *overtones* to give himself all the notes necessary for bugle calls. All brass instruments work in this manner.

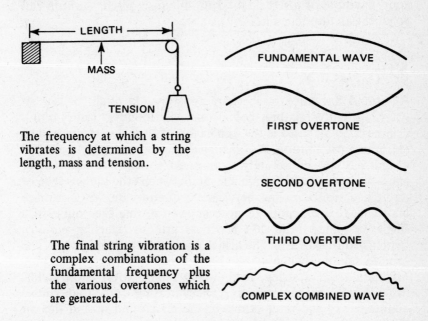

The frequency at which a string vibrates is determined by the length, mass and tension.

The final string vibration is a complex combination of the fundamental frequency plus the various overtones which are generated.

FIGURE 5

We call the number of harmonics present, and the relative strength of each harmonic in relation to the fundamental, the *spectrum* of a given note on a given instrument. Although this spectrum varies from one violin to another, and from one violinist to another, the variation is so confined that we would never mistake a violin for an oboe. Each instrument has its characteristic spectrum by which it can be identified. The more sophisticated the instrument, the greater its ability to vary color, and the better suited it is for complex musical expression. The human voice is a prime example of an instrument capable of a wide range of color changes.

If a series of unrelated fundamental pitches is produced simultaneously, each with its own overtone series, we no longer hear a distinct pitch. Our ears receive this as *noise*. Any solid, when struck, produces a series of sounds related to its own *natural resonant frequency*. The greater the mass of the solid, the lower the natural resonant frequency. Depending on the character of the solid, the natural resonant frequency may be a complex of fundamentals producing a noise, or it may be a single frequency and therefore produce a musical tone. A bell is a good example of a struck solid producing a pitch. An iron rail produces an unpitched noise.

Summary

All sound has three basic characteristics: (1) pitch (or lack of it); (2) quality (timbre, color); and (3) loudness (amplitude). Common to all three is the dimension of time, i.e. the period of existence, or duration. Within a given period of time (1) pitched sound may move discretely from one frequency to another, or glide through all the frequencies in between (the same is true of unpitched noise moving between frequency areas); (2) timbre may change from note to note or even during the course of a single sustained note; (3) loudness attacks (starting period), sustains (duration after the attack), and decays (dying out). The sound generated when a solid body is driven into vibration may originate from a string, reed, wood block, vocal chords, lips, drum head, loudspeaker, etc. The vibrating body then causes compressions and rarefactions in the air around it, and this air becomes the conducting medium to the receiver—either human ears or a microphone.

Some of the sound is heard directly, from the generating source to our ears. Sound moving out from the generating source may be reflected from the hard surfaces of a room, or it may bounce around many times before reaching the ear. These reflected sounds have traveled a greater distance than the sound reaching the ear directly, so they will be heard with a time delay, as well as at a lesser volume. This is called an echo; a combination of many echoes at different times is called reverberation. Reverberation also includes any sound characteristics that might be added or subtracted from the original sound by the reflecting surface itself, through filtering or sympathetic resonance.

The quality (timbre) of sound is determined by the overtone spectrum generated by the vibrating body. The ear can identify familiar sounds by their timbre. If the sound is a pitched conventional musical sound, the harmonics (overtones) tend to be related in a ratio of small whole numbers. If the fundamental tone (the lowest tone heard) has a frequency of 220 Hz., the first natural overtone (one octave higher) is 440 Hz., or double the frequency of the fundamental. The second overtone is in the ratio of 3:2 to the first overtone, and each successive overtone would be in a ratio of small, whole numbers.

Sound results from an oscillating wave motion which we can hear if it has a frequency of roughly 20 to 15,000 Hz. A vibrating body in an elastic transmitting medium such as air causes a series of compressions and rarefactions. The amount of energy with which the vibrating body generates these compressions and rarefactions determines the amplitude (loudness) of the sound. The degree of loudness is measured in exponential units called decibels (db). A basic understanding of sound and its transmission is essential to the comprehension of music as well as electronic instruments.

2. The Electronic Generation of Sound

The understanding, generation and use of electricity are recent developments in the history of man. A hundred or so years ago the world was without many of the things which we take for granted every day. The conversion of electrical energy into mechanical energy (an electric motor), conversion into light energy (an electric light bulb or an electric arc) and the conversion to sound energy (a loudspeaker or earphones) are all comparatively new.

We can describe *electricity* as a flow of energy (the movement of *electrons).* Certain materials, because of their atomic composition, allow electrons to flow through them quite easily. They are called *conductors.* Other materials, which resist the flow of electrons through them, are called *insulators.* Rubber is an example of a good insulator. A patch cord, which we use to interconnect various pieces of electronic equipment, is a combination of conductor and insulator. It consists of a piece of copper wire, which is a very good conductor, covered with rubber or plastic, both good insulators.

A generator, such as those in a powerhouse, which supplies us with household electricity, is, in effect, an electron pump. It converts mechanical energy into electrical energy by "pumping" electrons into a copper wire. If this wire is not connected to anything, it will build up a *voltage.* This is a force measured in terms of a unit called a *volt,* after Allessandro Volta (1745-1827), the great Italian physicist upon whom the title of Count was bestowed by Napoleon. But since these extra electrons have no place to go, they cannot flow. They simply remain there in a dormant state called a *potential,* which is similar to that of water in a hose with the nozzle turned off. However, if we provide a second wire through which the electrons can flow back to the generator, then we have an electric *current.* If the electrons are made to flow through a *transducer* (which is a device to convert one form of energy into another), we can produce heat energy, mechanical energy, light energy, or sound energy. Remember, there must always be a way for the electrons to get back to their source, the generator.

For example, suppose that we have to replace a light bulb. It has burned out, which really means that the wire (the filament) inside the glass bulb has finally separated and therefore broken the return path to the generator. We take a new bulb with the filament intact. As we begin to screw the bulb into the socket, the base of the bulb makes contact with the body of the socket. The bulb will not light since we have not yet provided a return path for the electrons. As the bulb is screwed in farther, the pin at the base of the bulb makes contact with the second wire. The electrons now have a complete and continuous path from the generator through the filament and back to the generator, and the bulb will light.

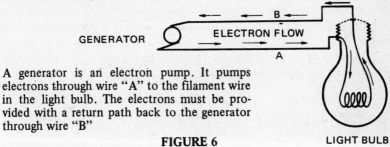

A generator is an electron pump. It pumps electrons through wire "A" to the filament wire in the light bulb. The electrons must be provided with a return path back to the generator through wire "B"

FIGURE 6

As a more dangerous example, suppose by accident you touch one element of the socket. If no part of your body is touching a conductor you will not be harmed because electrons cannot flow through your body. If you happen to be touching a conductor, such as a water pipe, the electrons can flow through your body and you will experience a shock. This is why birds can sit on a high tension power line and not be electrocuted: since they are not touching a conductor, they do not provide a return path for the electrons back to the generator (Figure 6).

A. Direct Current and Alternating Current

If the electrons always flow through a conductor in the same direction, we call this *direct current* (DC). However, if the generator produces a flow of electrons which move through a conductor first in one direction and then in the opposite direction, we call it *alternating current* (AC). Whether we have direct or alternating current is determined by the generating source. Most household electric current is AC, but we do have electrical converters which will change AC to DC or DC to AC.

We express the flow of electrons in a unit called an *ampere*, named after the famous French physicist, André Marie Ampère (1775-1836). Normal household electricity is usually 240 volts, AC. The number of times that the electrons change direction in alternating current is measured in cycles per second (Hz.). Normal household electicity changes direction 50 times a second, which is how the generators are constructed, so we can now describe the electricity as 240 volts (the potential), AC (alternating current) and 5 Hz. (cycles per second). Alternating current electricity can be generated at much higher frequencies. We encounter this in our AM radios, which are calibrated in kilocycles (kilohertz), or thousands of cycles per second. FM radios are calibrated in megacycles (megahertz), which means millions of cycles per second. In radio transmission to the moon frequencies even higher are used.

B. Electricity and Magnetism

Many centuries ago man discovered a peculiar type of rock, one that had the ability to attract certain metals to it. The rock was called a *lodestone*—iron ore that becomes magnetic from a mysterious force of nature which is known as *magnetism*. Though this force has been recognized, and ways have been found to use it, it is not yet fully understood and remains virtually indefinable. The lodestone was an important discovery, because when it was suspended so that it could rotate freely, it would always end up pointing north and south. As an aid to navigation it was invaluable. It is the basis of the sophisticated versions in use today. It is, of course, the compass. Later it was discovered that there is a direct relationship between electricity and magnetism. If a compass is brought close to a wire through which DC current is flowing, the needle will turn toward the wire, indicating that the flow of electricity is producing a magnetic field. Conversely, if a wire is passed through a magnetic field, an electrical current will be induced into the wire.

Instead of a single wire, suppose we wrap many turns of wire around an iron core. When we run a current through the wire, the magnetic field is proportionately stronger. If we take our coil of wire and pass it through a magnetic field, the current generated will be stronger in proportion to how many turns of wire there are in the coil. In fact, our first example above is called an *electromagnet,* and our second is actually a generator. Most electricity is generated by the same system: a coil of wire

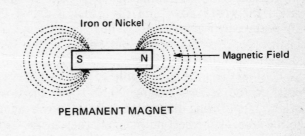

Iron or Nickel

S   N   Magnetic Field

PERMANENT MAGNET

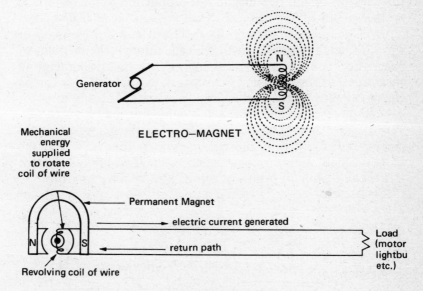

Generator

Mechanical
energy
supplied
to rotate
coil of wire

ELECTRO—MAGNET

Permanent Magnet

electric current generated

return path

Load
(motor
lightbu
etc.)

Revolving coil of wire

THE GENERATOR

Permanent Magnet

electric current

return path

generator
supplies
electrical
energy

coil of wire

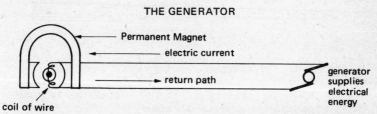

mechanical energy is produced as coil of wire rotates due to magnetism.

THE ELECTRIC MOTOR

FIGURE 7

is passed through a magnetic field. If we wrap our wire around a piece of iron, which is a magnetic metal, it concentrates the magnetic fields of force so that our electromagnet becomes even more powerful (Figure 7).

There are two dissimilar ends to our magnet. One end is called the *north pole,* and the other is called the *south pole.* Since the earth is, in effect, a huge magnet, we also refer to the earth's ends as the north and south poles. If we bring two magnets together with like poles facing each other, they repel each other, i.e. the north pole of one magnet repels the north pole of the second magnet. The south poles also repel each other. If we bring the north pole of one magnet close to the south pole of the second magnet, they attract with the sum of the strength of the two magnets in proportion to the reciprocal of the square of the distance. Thus we can say that *like poles repel,* and *opposites attract.* By mechanically moving a coil of wire through a magnetic field, we can, through the medium of magnetism, convert mechanical energy into electrical energy (a *generator*), or, by reversing the process, electrical energy can be converted into mechanical energy (a *motor*). Actually a motor may be used as a generator, and a generator may be used as a motor, since both consist basically of a fixed magnet and a moving coil of wire. If the coil of wire is rotated within the fixed magnetic field, we have a generator. If we apply a current to the coil of wire, it begins to rotate, and we have a motor.

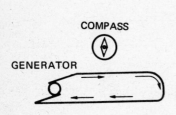

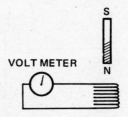

A compass needle is deflected toward a wire which is conducting DC current, showing that a magnetic field has been created around the conducting wire.

Conversely, when a magnet is moved near a coil of wire which is connected to a volt meter, the volt meter shows that a current has been generated.

FIGURE 8

It is very important to understand the nature of magnetism and electricity, since in electronic music, we have to convert electricity into audible sound through the medium of magnetism (Figure 8).

C. Magnetism and the Loudspeaker

We can divide magnets into two basic classes: (1) *permanent magnets,* where certain metals such as iron and nickel can be permanently magnetized by being placed in a strong magnetic field, and (2) *electromagnets,* where a current passing through a coil of wire induces magnetism into a core of iron or nickel. We have found that the direction of flow of electricity through a coil of wire determines where the north pole will be. If we reverse the flow of electricity through the coil, the north and south poles will reverse in position. It is on this principle that we can construct a loudspeaker.

Basically, a loudspeaker is a transducer (remember, a transducer is a device to convert one form of energy into another) which converts electrical energy to sound energy (which is mechanical) through the intermediary of magnetic energy. Suppose that we take a permanent magnet and attach it rigidly to a frame so that it can't vibrate. Let us put a coil of insulated electric wire loosely around the end of the permanent magnet so that it, on the other hand, can vibrate. If we now apply an alternating current to the loose coil of wire, one end will become a north pole and will be attracted to the permanent magnet. But now the alternating current reverses direction, and our north pole becomes a south pole. The current now moves in the opposite direction, and the coil moves in the opposite direction, since it is repelled by a like pole of the permanent magnet. As the current alternates, so do the poles, and the coil is alternately attracted and repelled in exact step with the alternating current being passed through it. In order to amplify mechanically the volume of air moved by the coil, the coil is usually glued to a conical piece of cardboard or thin sheet metal. This is essentially all there is to a loudspeaker. In sound reproduction there are many variations in types of speakers; each speaker has its own qualities. The diameter of the coil, the diameter of the cone, the strength of the magnet, and the materials used may all vary, but all are essentially a fixed magnet plus a magnet that is free to vibrate (Figure 9).

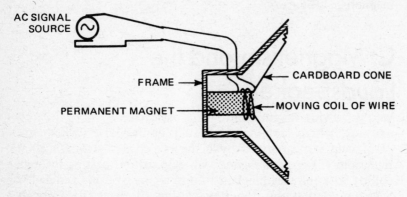

In a loudspeaker, the alternating current (AC) flows through a coil of wire which changes its polarity as the current changes. Since the coil of wire is suspended over one pole of a permanent magnet, its changing polarity will alternately draw it toward the magnet and repel away from the magnet in step with the AC. The cardboard cone, which is attached to the moving coil, amplifies the movement of the coil mechanically.

FIGURE 9

D. Magnetism and the Microphone

Just as we have seen that a motor has basically the same construction as a generator, so a loudspeaker has basically the same construction as a microphone. A microphone is a transducer which converts sound wave energy into electrical energy. A *dynamic* type microphone is basically a fixed permanent magnet with a freely moving coil of wire over one end. A cone or diaphragm concentrates the sound energy and makes the coil of wire move in step with the incoming vibrations. As the coil moves in one direction over the permanent magnet an electrical current is induced in the same direction; as the coil moves in the opposite direction the current flows in the reverse direction, resulting in an alternating current directly reflecting the sound vibrations. Of course, in the recording studio we also use a number of more sophisticated types of microphone, but for the time being, let us stay with the dynamic microphone.

E. The Amplifier

An *amplifier* is a device which takes a form of energy and raises it to a higher level (order) of the same form of energy. In other words, if we take a very low voltage output from our dynamic microphone, we can amplify this voltage so that instead of being a few hundredths of a volt AC, it can be built up into a number of volts AC which exactly parallel the incoming voltage. Thus we can take a few millivolts (thousandths of a volt) from a studio microphone and, by passing them through an audio amplifier, build them up to be thousands of times more powerful in order to drive a loudspeaker. The increase in power, of amplifier output over input to the amplifier, is the *amplification factor*. It was observed by Sir Isaac Newton (1642-1727) that matter and energy can neither be created nor destroyed. For this reason any additional energy needed in the system must be added from an external source. This is done with a *power supply* which usually takes line current (the normal 117 volts AC) and uses it to build up the incoming low voltage from the microphone. This low voltage from the microphone is called the *signal*. Since it leaves the generating source (the microphone), it is called the *output* of the microphone. The point at which the signal is injected into the amplifier is called the *input* of the amplifier; where the higher level signal leaves the amplifier to go to the loudspeaker is the *output* of the amplifier. Where the stepped-up signal from the amplifier goes into the loudspeaker is called the *input* of the loudspeaker. This converts the electrical energy into sound energy, which is called the loudspeaker *output*. In tracing our signal it is important to understand that as it leaves one device it is called an *output* and that as it enters the next device it is called an *input*. An amplifier, then, raises the level of input energy to a higher level of the same form of energy (in this case, electrical) at its output by means of an external energy source called a power supply (Figure 10).

In the design of audio amplifiers (amplifiers which increase the amplitude between 20 and 15,000 Hz. of the AC voltages) we try to get the output signal to resemble the input signal as closely as possible in all ways except amplitude. The more closely the output signal of the amplifier resembles the input signal, the higher the *fidelity*. Fidelity means faithfulness, therefore "high fidelity" has to do with the degree of faithfulness with which the original sound is reproduced and/or amplified. The changes that may result from the faulty design of an amplifier is called *distortion*—that is, the input of the amplifier does not compare very well with the output. The higher the fidelity, the lower the distortion. The trade-off in

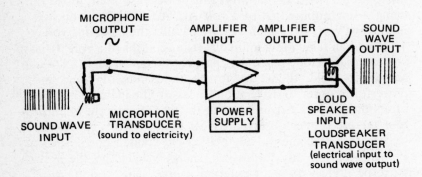

Each electrical system has an input and an output. The sound wave input is converted by the microphone into an electrical output. This low power output becomes the amplifier input which is boosted by the amplifier to a level that can operate a loudspeaker. This boosted signal becomes the input to the loudspeaker which converts the electrical energy back into an amplified sound wave output.

FIGURE 10

amplifier design is between fidelity and power. Usually, we have to compromise and decrease the power factor in order to achieve better fidelity. In a public address system, however, where a great amount of audio power is needed, fidelity is generally sacrificed.

In some types of sound amplification it has become customary to introduce a degree of distortion intentionally. An amplifier can be designed to distort by over-driving some of its components. For example, in an electric guitar amplifier, a fairly high distortion factor is added on purpose to give the instrument its characteristic "electric guitar" sound. The "fuzz tone" sound is achieved by a special amplifier with a built-in high distortion factor.

A very important test instrument which we use to check distortion is an *oscilloscope*. It is a transducer that converts electrical energy into light energy. The input is our AC signal;

the output is a trace on a screen (similar to a television tube) of the wave shape of the input AC signal. We can connect the oscilloscope to the output of the amplifier and compare the two wave shapes. If they are substantially the same, we say that we have high fidelity to the input signal; if the wave shape is different visually, we say we have distortion.

F. The Audio Oscillator

Since the audio oscillator is the basic sound-generating source of a synthesizer, an understanding of how it works is important. If you look closely at a plucked string on a violin, you can see it vibrating and therefore setting up sound waves in the air. The rate of speed at which the string vibrates is the result of the length of the string, tension in the string, and the mass (weight) of the material of which the string is made. This is a *mechanical oscillator*. An *audio oscillator* is an AC generator whose output voltage changes at a frequency of roughly 20 Hz. to 15,000 Hz. It can be designed to produce the desired frequencies by varying the components used in its construction.

In most electronic organs, there is a separate oscillator for each of the 12 highest chromatic tones, and divider circuits (to be described later) are used to generate the lower octaves of the keyboard. These oscillators are designed to be very stable in pitch, while on most synthesizers the oscillators are designed so that they can change pitch easily. On an organ keyboard, as we depress each key, we are using a different oscillator. On a synthesizer, as we depress each key (on those that have keyboards), a single oscillator changes pitch according to the key depressed. This is one of the basic differences between an electronic organ and a synthesizer: the synthesizer has variable-pitch rather than fixed-pitch oscillators.

Suppose we take an audio amplifier and connect a microphone to the input and a loudspeaker to the output. This is basically a public address system. If we place the microphone too close to the loudspeaker, it will pick up whatever sound there is in the room and pass it through the amplifier, which in turn will pass this amplified sound on to the loudspeaker. However, since the microphone is close to the loudspeaker, it will pick up the amplified sound and once again pass it on through the amplifier to the loudspeaker. Each time this happens it gets louder and louder until either the amplifying capacity of the amplifier is reached or the speaker burns out. We have all been in an auditorium when this situation has occurred and the public address (PA) system has howled. We call this effect *feedback,* since a signal is repeatedly fed back to itself through an amplifier.

We do basically the same thing with the audio oscillator. We eliminate the microphone and speaker, and simply connect the output of the amplifier, through proper circuitry, to the input. A *circuit* is a combination of interconnected electronic components. Depending on the components in the feedback circuit, the oscillator will oscillate at a specific frequency which we call the *resonant frequency.* If we change the components in the feedback circuit, a different resonant frequency will result. In an audio oscillator this resonant frequency is in the audible range between 20 Hz. and 15,000 Hz. Oscillators, of course, are made with the capacity to produce frequencies of many millions of cycles per second, but these are in the radio frequencies which cannot be heard. Essentially, these oscillators work in the same way as audio oscillators; only the feedback network is changed. If you recall in our discussion of audio amplifiers, additional power had to be added to the system from a power supply. If we add the right amount of power from the power supply, the amplifier's amplification factor will be greater. If we add too much power, however, the distortion factor will increase. If we change the power input to an oscillator, the frequency will change. Depending on the design, the shape of the output wave form can also be altered by changing the power input. Therefore, if we want a stable oscillator, we must have a very stable power supply. In the synthesizer these are most important elements, and we will discuss them in more detail later.

G. The Filter

A *filter* is a device which selectively allows certain frequencies present in a signal to pass through it, while stopping others. A sieve is a form of mechanical filter. It allows water to pass through it, but keeps the spaghetti from falling into the sink. The telephone is a voice filter. Many of the frequencies generated by your speaking voice are not passed through the system, because fidelity to your true vocal sound is not needed for vocal exchange of information. *Mutes* for the trumpet or violin are mechanical filters, since they pass certain frequencies and eliminate others.

In electronic music we use filters which act directly on the alternating current electrical signal rather than using mechanical filters on the sound waves eventually produced. A *band* of frequencies refers to all of the frequencies contained between specified lower and upper limits. For instance, we already know that the audio band of frequencies has a lower limit of around 20 Hz. and an upper limit of about 15,000 Hz. The band of frequencies that a telephone might pass would be between about 300 and 3,000 Hz. A filter that will pass a certain band is called a *band pass filter,* since it will pass this band of frequencies and reject the rest. An inverse of this filter is a *band reject filter,* designed to reject a specific band of frequencies. Suppose that we had to do a *remote recording* session. This

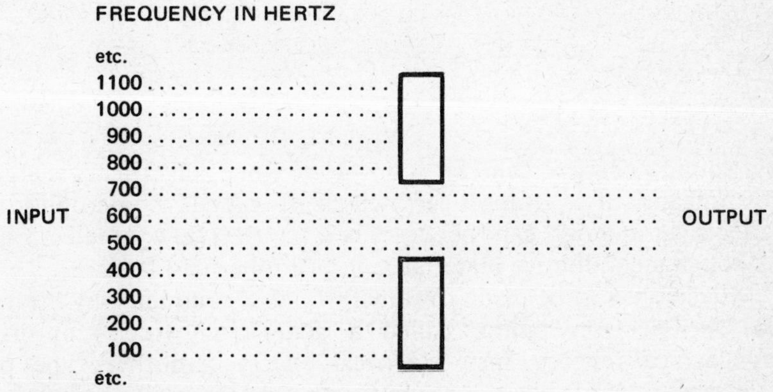

FREQUENCY IN HERTZ

```
          etc.
          1100 . . . . . . . . . . . . . . . . . . . . . .
          1000 . . . . . . . . . . . . . . . . . . . . . .
           900 . . . . . . . . . . . . . . . . . . . . .
           800 . . . . . . . . . . . . . . . . . . . . .
           700 . . . . . . . . . . . . . . . . . . . . . . . . . . . . . . . . . . . . . . . . . . . . . . . . . . .
INPUT      600 . . . . . . . . . . . . . . . . . . . . . . . . . . . . . . . . . . . . . . . . . . . . . . . .     OUTPUT
           500 . . . . . . . . . . . . . . . . . . . . . . . . . . . . . . . . . . . . . . . . . . . .
           400 . . . . . . . . . . . . . . . . . . . . .
           300 . . . . . . . . . . . . . . . . . . . .
           200 . . . . . · . . . . . . . . . . . . . .
           100 . . . . . . . . . . . . . . . . . . . .
          etc.
```

A band pass filter made to pass a bandwidth of frequencies between 500 and 700 Hz.

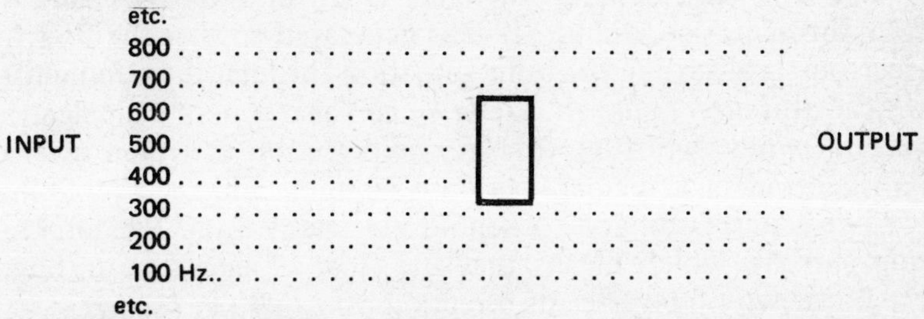

```
          etc.
           800 . . . . . . . . . . . . . . . . . . . . . . . . . . . . . . . . . . . . . . . . . . . . . .
           700 . . . . . . . . . . . . . . . . . . . . . . . . . . . . . . . . . . . . . . . . . . . . . .
           600 . . . . . . . . . . . . . . . . . . . . . . .
INPUT      500 . . . . . . . . . . . . . . . . . . . . .                                                         OUTPUT
           400 . . . . . . . . . . . . . . . . . .
           300 . . . . . . . . . . . . . . . . . . . . . . . . . . . . . . . . . . . . . . . . . . . .
           200 . . . . . . . . . . . . . . . . . . . . . . . . . . . . . . . . . . . . . . . . . . . .
           100 Hz.. . . . . . . . . . . . . . . . . . . . . . . . . . . . . . . . . . . . . . . . . . .
          etc.
```

A band reject filter made to reject all frequencies in the 300 to 700 Hz. band, but to pass all other frequencies.

FIGURE 11

means a recording session away from a recording studio, "on location." We find that where we are recording, certain street sounds can be heard which are objectionable, such as a passing bus or automobile. To get rid of this low frequency rumble of the bus we use a filter which rejects any frequency, say, below 100 Hz. This will not affect the quality of the voice recording we wish to do, but it will eliminate the possibility of recording the low frequency rumble of the bus or car.

We usually divide filters into two general classes: *high pass filters* and *low pass filters*. A high pass filter is designed to pass higher frequencies and reject the lower. A low pass filter is designed to pass low frequencies and reject the higher. Filters are very important for changing the quality and timbre of an intial sound. Since a filter can change the *harmonic structure* (which refers to the overtones that are present in a sound), it is a most useful device, both for synthesizing the sounds of conventional instruments and for creating entirely new sounds (Figure 11).

Summary

Sound energy can be converted into electrical energy by means of a transducer, which is called a microphone. Electrical energy can be described as the flow of electrons through a conductive material such as copper or silver.

Electrons can be made to flow through a conductor by means of an electron pump, called a generator, which converts mechanical energy into electrical energy. Another type of electron pump is a battery, which converts chemical energy into electrical energy.

This flow of electrons—the electric current—can be made to flow through a conductor. If it is generated so that the flow of electrons is always in the same direction through the conductor, we call this *direct current (DC)*. We can also generate an electric current, which will flow first in one direction and then reverse its direction in a regular, periodic manner. This is *alternating current (AC)*. Ordinary household electricity is 50 Hz. alternating current, which means that the flow of electrons through the house wiring reverses its direction 50 times per second.

Electric current and magnetism are inseparable. Whenever an electric current flows through a conductor, a magnetic field is generated. The polarity (where the north and south poles lie) of the magnetic field is determined by the direction of flow of this electric current. If the electric current changes its direction of flow, say at 50 times a second, the alternating current will produce a magnetic field that will change its polarity 60 times a second.

Conversely, if a conductor (like a wire) is passed through a magnetic field, an electric current will be induced into the conductor. The direction of flow of this induced electric current will be determined by the polarity of the magnetic field and by the direction of movement of the conductor. However, in order for the electric current to flow, a complete path must be provided to carry the electrons away from the generating source to the load (whatever the electricity is to operate); then a return path must be provided for the electrons to return to the generating source. This is called a complete circuit, which means that a complete electrical path has been provided for the electrons—to the generator and away from the generator. Any interruption (such as by a switch) in a complete circuit will cause the flow of electrons to stop.

Certain metals such as iron, nickel, and cobalt can be magnetized. The earth itself, with a primarily iron core, is a magnet with a north pole and south pole. A characteristic of all magnets is that opposite poles attract. A north pole of a magnet will attract a south pole. Like poles repel. A south pole will repel another south pole and a north pole will repel another north pole.

Electric motors and loudspeakers are based on this principle. A fixed magnet, called a *pole piece,* is mounted firmly on a frame. A coil of wire is mounted close to the pole piece, but in such a way that it can rotate (go around) in the case of a motor, or oscillate (move back and forth) in the case of a loudspeaker. When an alternating current passes through the coil of wire, it is alternately attracted and repelled by the magnet of the pole piece, thus causing the coil to move. In a loudspeaker the moving coil of wire is usually glued to a cardboard cone in order to move a greater volume of air. The entire loudspeaker is often mounted inside a specially designed box which is intended to improve the efficiency of the loudspeaker.

If we reverse the above procedure and mechanically move a coil of wire in and out of a magnetic field, an electric current will be induced into the wire. If the coil of wire is revolving within a magnetic field, we call this a generator. If the coil of wire is moving back and forth in a magnetic field, we call this a dynamic microphone.

An amplifier is a device that raises a form of energy to a higher level of the same form of energy. An *audio amplifier* (an amplifier designed to increase the energy level of alternating current electrical signals from 15 Hz. to 15,000 Hz.) can take the relatively weak electrical signals generated from a microphone and build them up to a high enough level to operate a loudspeaker. The energy that is added must come from another source—the power supply, which furnishes the additional electrical power needed to raise the weak audio signals to a strong signal.

When we compare signals coming into an amplifier with the output signal of the amplifier, we can say that we have high fidelity when the signals are the same in all respects except the amplitude (loudness or strength). *Distortion* occurs when the output signal has been altered. This distortion can be measured and is usually stated as a percentage, which indicates the degree of distortion in comparison with the true signal.

Where any form of signal enters a device, whether it is a transducer (microphone) or an amplifier, we call this the *input*. Where the signal leaves a device, it is an *output*. Therefore, the input to the microphone is sound energy. The output is electrical energy, which should be an analog to the sound energy input. This output then becomes the input to the amplifier, which raises the energy level of the incoming signal. The output of the amplifier then becomes the input of the loudspeaker, which, as a transducer, converts the electrical energy back into sound energy. This is the output of the loudspeaker.

If the output of an amplifier is returned to the input of the amplifier, it is *feedback,* and the amplifier will begin to generate an oscillating electric current. It has, in effect, become an AC generator. The frequency of oscillations can be determined by the circuitry, which connects the output of the amplifier to its input. The power supply can also control the frequency of the oscillations. We call this type of amplifier an *oscillator*; if the frequency of oscillations is in the audible spectrum (15 Hz. to 15,000 Hz.), it is an audio oscillator. This is the basic sound generator in almost all electronic musical instruments. In organs, these oscillators are designed to be fixed in frequency; there is usually an oscillator for each chromatic note in the scale. In a synthesizer, the oscillators are designed to be variable in frequency, depending on a controlling voltage, which tells the oscillator at what frequency to oscillate.

A filter is a device that separates one thing from another. An air filter in an air conditioner separates the dust from the air. An audio filter separates a group of audio frequencies from another. These groups of audio frequencies are called *bands;* we can specify which frequencies these bands will encompass. For example, we can designate a band of 100 Hz. to 300 Hz., which would include all of the frequencies between 100 and 300 Hz.

Audio filters are generally divided into two groups: a high pass filter, which likes to pass higher frequencies and to reject lower frequencies; and a low pass filter, which prefers to pass low-frequency bands and which rejects higher frequency bands. The tone controls on a hi-fi phonograph are good examples of high-pass and low-pass filters. Filters are extremely important for the modification of the quality and character of sound. With filters we can selectively rebalance the overtones of a complex tone to change its character and quality. The drawbars and stops on electric organs other than the Hammond activate filters that change the character of the complex tone generated by the oscillators. On the synthesizer, filters are extremely important; the bands of frequencies these filters will pass can often be varied. This is commonly used for wa-wa effects and many other interesting sounds. These filters are discussed later.

3. The Recording of Sound

A. Mechanical Recording

Thomas A. Edison (1847-1931) invented the phonograph, and to this day our disc recordings are based on the Edison invention. He knew that sound waves could set a thin piece of metal into vibration by *sympathetic resonance*. He reasoned that if a stylus (needle) were attached to the sheet of metal (called a diaphragm), and if this, in turn, were pressed against a soft material that could be embossed, a pattern of sound vibrations could be traced onto the soft material. The material he used at first was tin foil which he wrapped around a rotating drum. Later it was found that shellac could be embossed more easily, and today, vinyl is used.

When the process was reversed, and the drum embossed with the sound pattern forced the stylus into vibration, the diaphragm was forced into vibration, and the sound pattern was converted back into sound waves which reproduced a simulation of the original signal.

In the production of the modern phonograph recording we have replaced the mechanical amplifier (the diaphragm) with electronic amplifiers. These amplifiers, driving a coil and permanent magnet similar to a loudspeaker, move a stylus which cuts the sound pattern into a master recording disc. This disc is then electroplated with copper and nickel, which, when it is removed, becomes a shell or mold. It is then filled with metal to strengthen it, and it becomes a negative of the original master disc. It is then used as a stamper to impress the sound patterns onto heated plastic in order to "mold" or "press" copies of the finished record.

B. Optical Recording

Eventually, other types of recording were developed. *Optical recording* was developed for use with photographic film, which made it possible for sound to be synchronized with motion picture action. Incidentally, Edison also invented the motion picture camera and performed many experiments in attempting to coordinate his phonograph with his motion picture projector.

In optical recording, sound waves are converted into electrical energy in the usual way—with a microphone. This signal is then amplified through an audio amplifier and once again passes into a coil arranged around a permanent magnet. The vibrating coil, rather than being attached to a cardboard cone as it is in a loudspeaker, is attached to an *iris*. Modeled after the eye, the iris is a mechanical device that allows varying amounts of light to pass through it. This varying light beam, when focused onto a strip of moving picture film, exposes the film to a greater or lesser degree, depending on the aperture of the iris. The film is then developed and the results are varying bands of light and dark sections which parallel the original variations in the sound pattern. This is called a *sound track*. If you examine a piece of motion picture film, you will see the sound track running along the edge. Its position is such that when run through the projector, the *sound head*, which converts light patterns back into electrical fluctuations, will produce the sound in synchronization with the picture. The sound head consists of a light beam which passes through the sound track portion of the film and falls onto a *photoconductive cell*. This cell contains a special chemical which allows varying amounts of electricity to pass through it, depending on how much light strikes its surface. The *density* (the degree of lightness and darkness of the film) allows varying amounts of light to pass onto the photoconductive cell, and the *photocell* produces an electrical fluctuation in step with the sound track. This varying current is then amplified and converted into sound waves by a loudspeaker.

Of course, there are many variations and systems for recording sound optically, but basically they are all variations of the system we have described. Since a great deal of original music is written for film, it is important to know some of the steps that are taken to convert the composer's thoughts into audible sounds.

C. Magnetic Recording

Although the idea of using varying magnetic force to record sound patterns had been around for a good many years, it was not developed into a practical concept until the early 1940's. Magnetic tape has become the most practical recording method now available. We know that we can create a fluctuating electrical force by converting sound waves into electrical impulses, using a microphone as a transducer. These electrical impulses can then be converted into proportionately varying magnetic impulses by using an electromagnet as the transducer. Furthermore, we know that we can magnetize certain metals and metal oxides to varying degrees. These are the basic principles of *magnetic sound recording.*

The tape used is usually a mylar or acetate ribbon (similar to Scotch Tape), which is coated on one side with a magnetizable material such as iron oxide. This is bonded to the tape with a very strong adhesive. If you look at a piece of recording tape, you will notice one side is shiny (the acetate), while the other is dull (the iron oxide, a chemical commonly known as rust). When we record, we always have to make sure that the dull oxide side comes into contact with the recording head, and not the other way around. The tape is supplied on metal or plastic reels. The three most common size reels are 5″, 7″ and 10½″ in diameter. In the recording studio we generally use 10½″ reels. Naturally, the larger the diameter of the reels, the more tape that can be wound on it and therefore, the longer time it will take to run through the tape recorder, and the more material that can be recorded. The tape comes in different thicknesses for different uses. Thickness is measured in mils (thousandths of an inch); standard tape is available in thickness of ½ mil, 1 mil and 1½ mil. In the studio 1½ mil is usually used, since it is stronger and more durable. Tape also comes in various widths. For a tape cassette, ⅛″ wide tape is used. In the studio we use ¼″ for 1- and 2-track recording, ½″ tape for 4-track recording, 1″ tape for 8- and 12-track recording and 2″ tape for 16-track recording. We will discuss "tracks" later.

COMPONENTS OF THE TAPE RECORDER

1. *The Transport Mechanism* consists of one or more motors mounted on a solid metal plate called a *deck.* Their purpose is to move the tape at a highly constant speed past the recording and playback heads (which we will describe soon). The standard tape speeds used in the studio are 7½ and 15 inches per second (IPS). The faster the tape is moved, the better the recording quality. On home tape recorders slower speeds are usually used in order to consume less tape. The average home tape recorder transports the tape at 7½ IPS or 3¾ IPS, or occasionally at 1⅞ IPS for recording speech where fidelity is not a big factor. Notice that all of the speeds mentioned are in the relationship

of one-half of the next higher speed—15, 7½, 3¾ and 1⅞ IPS.

The transport mechanism also provides mechanical power for a *feed reel* which supplies fresh tape, and a *take-up reel* which winds up the tape after it has gone past the recording and playback heads. Sometimes we want to move the tape rapidly from the feed reel to the take-up reel. In order to wind the tape back onto the supply reel, a reverse position is also available, called *rewind*, which rapidly moves the tape backward to the supply reel. On professional studio recorders, there are separate motors for each of these three functions. The motor that moves the tape at a constant speed when we are recording or playing back is called the *capstan motor*. The tape is pressed against the rotating shaft of the capstan motor by a *pressure roller* which is usually made of rubber. The *take-up motor* keeps a constant tension on the tape after it passes the capstan motor and winds the tape up after it has passed the recording and playback heads. This same motor runs at a more rapid speed in the fast forward mode, during which time the capstan motor disengages from the tape. The *rewind motor* is attached to the rewind reel and is used to rewind the tape rapidly.

Since it is most important that the tape be drawn past the record and playback heads at a very constant speed, a heavy flywheel and/or an electronic speed control is used. Various electronic devices may be used to keep the capstan motor speed as steady as possible. Lack of speed stability will cause the tape to be drawn past the heads at varying speeds, with resultant small variations in pitch called *flutter*. Naturally, on studio recorders this flutter must be kept as low as possible, and a variety of speed-stabilizing devices are used. One of these is the *tension arm*. This is a spring-loaded arm over which the tape must pass, and the spring tension helps to stabilize the speed. It is usually equipped with a switch so that when there is no more tape passing over the arm, it springs back to a rest position and turns off all of the motors in the transport. Mechanical brakes are also built into the tape transport to stop the reels rapidly when desired (Figure 12).

2. *The Control Mechanism* is built onto the transport mechanism. It consists of a series of function switches and buttons, as follows:

(a) *STOP* This is an important function, as you well imagine. We also call it the "panic button." It stops all of the transport motors and applies the brakes to the reels.

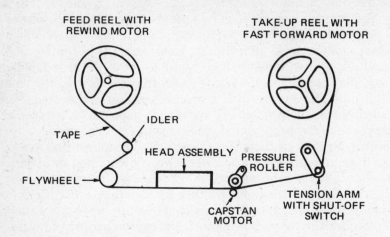

FEED REEL WITH
REWIND MOTOR

TAKE-UP REEL WITH
FAST FORWARD MOTOR

IDLER

TAPE

HEAD ASSEMBLY PRESSURE
ROLLER

FLYWHEEL

TENSION ARM
WITH SHUT-OFF
SWITCH

CAPSTAN
MOTOR

Basic components of the tape recorder tape transport mechanism.

FIGURE 12

(b) *PLAY* This activates the transport motors and engages the pressure roller so that the capstan motor draws the tape past the heads at a constant speed and the take-up reel winds up the tape. It also activates the proper section of electronics needed to play back the signal recorded on the tape.

(c) *RECORD* This important button is usually red and when depressed, turns on a light which indicates that the tape recorder is in the record mode. The same motors are activated as in PLAY; however, the record electronics are activated instead of the playback electronics. It is important to remember that when this button is depressed, any previously recorded material on the tape is automatically and permanently erased.

(d) *FAST FORWARD* When this button is depressed, the tape is wound rapidly from the feed reel to the take-up reel. The capstan motor is disengaged, and in order not to wear down the heads by abrasion, *tape lifters* are either manually or automatically engaged. The tape lifter is usually a set of metal arms which simply hold the moving tape away from the heads. If these are manually operated, usually by opening a "gate" over the heads, you should never forget to open the gate in fast forward and fast rewind modes. It will save excessive wear on the heads and will save your ears, since if there is material recorded on the tape, when it moves at such rapid speeds past the heads, it will produce a very loud sound, quite capable of blowing out your loudspeakers.

(e) *FAST REWIND* This moves the tape back from the take-up reel to the feed reel at a rapid rate. Remember the tape lifters!

(f) *EDIT* This button engages the "play" mode of operation so that the capstan motor engages the tape and draws it past the playback head. However, the take-up reel motor does not engage so that the tape is not wound up on the take-up reel but merely "spills." This is used for editing when a section of recorded tape is no good and you may wish to discard it. To do this you simply cut out the section to be discarded, then splice together the two loose ends of tape to be retained. These operations are best performed on a *splice block,* an aluminum channel into which the tape fits. There are slots cut into the channel to guide a razor blade. Be sure that the blade is not magnetized in any way! Each end of the tape to be spliced is cut at matching angles, the two ends are butted together, and a self-adhesive splicing tape is used to stick the two pieces of tape together. A properly made splice will not be heard as the tape passes the playback head.

(g) *SPEED* This is a speed selector switch which will change the tape speed on a studio machine from 7½ IPS to 15 IPS.

(h) *REEL SIZE* This is a set of switches used to balance the tape tension if you are using different reel sizes for a feed reel and a take-up reel. The control buttons and functions usually have an interlocking system so that the machine cannot be thrown into two opposing functions at the same time. Sometimes, if this system should be misused, or if it should fail, you can end up with 1,200 feet of tape on the floor (which might be the best part of your composition); so it pays to learn the various functions of the machine quite carefully, and with scrap tape.

3. *The Electronic Assembly* hereinafter referred to simply as "the electronics," consists of a series of amplifiers and oscillators. The *record amplifier* takes a low level voltage from the microphone and builds it up to the level needed to operate the electromagnet which records the magnetism on the tape. The *playback amplifier* takes the low level (voltage) signal that is generated as the tape passes over the playback magnet and builds it up to a level sufficient to operate a small loudspeaker or drive a large audio amplifier. The *bias oscillator* generates a high frequency oscillating electric current of around 100,000

Hz., well above the audible range. (We could write this as 100K Hz. "K" stands for "kilo" which means thousand.) How this is used will be explained later on.

There is often a *selector switch* incorporated into the electronic assembly. This is to select "input" into the electronics or "output" used to listen to what is going through the electronics.

A *level indicator* is provided in the form of a volt meter which has the lower portion calibrated from minus 20 db to 0 db and the upper portion, usually colored red, calibrated from 0 db to plus 3 db. When the selector switch is in "input" mode, it indicates the strength of the signal going to the record head. It is very important to record at the proper level. If we try to put too much signal on the tape, the tape will reach the saturation point beyond which it cannot be magnetized, and the result will be a high level of distortion. If we record at too low a level, the signal will be too faint to be heard above the *ambient* (background) noise level of the tape. We will discuss this "signal to noise" ratio later.

This indicator, or level meter, is called a *VU meter* and as the incoming signal varies it indicates the different levels. We try to average the level to be as close to the 0 db as we can. Occasional "peaking into the red" momentarily is acceptable, but if the needle should be "pinned" in the red, distortion is sure to result. The level controls on the electronics of the recorder or on the input source must be set to record at the proper level (Figure 13).

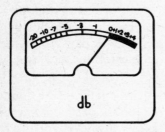

A level meter called a VU meter indicates the voltage going to the record head. It is calibrated in decibles.

FIGURE 13

4. *The Head Assembly* on a professional recorder consists of three separate electromagnets over which the tape must pass. The first head the tape comes in contact with is called the *erase head*. The bias oscillator in the electronics supplies this head

with 100K Hz. oscillating current. This is used to erase anything which may have been pre-recorded or any residual magnetism which might be on the tape. This operates only when the recorder is in the "record" mode. The tape then comes into contact with the *record head*. This is another electromagnet whose current comes from the record amplifier in the electronics. The signal we wish to record is converted into a parallel magnetic impulse which actually magnetizes the tape in varying strengths. This head, too, only functions when the tape recorder is in the "record" mode. The final electromagnetic head that the tape passes over is called the *playback head*. As the magnetized tape passes over this coil of wire it induces into the coil electrical impulses parallel to those which were used to record on the tape originally. The signal then goes to the playback amplifier where this signal is built up to a level that can operate a loudspeaker. On home tape recorders the record and playback function are sometimes combined in the same head, since a record head can function as a playback head. On professional machines, however, separate heads are used with a slightly different design to get the best possible fidelity (Figure 14).

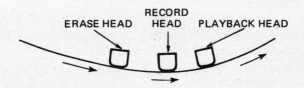

The tape is drawn past an erase head, which erases any magnetism which may be on the tape. It then passes the record head electromagnet which records on the tape. The magnetized tape then passes over the playback head coil which then converts the magnetism back into an electrical signal.

FIGURE 14

D. Multi-track Recording

So far we have discussed a single piece of tape passing over a single set of heads; erase, record and playback. But suppose we constructed the heads narrow enough so that we would record only on the top half of the width of the tape. If we could provide our machine with another set of heads, built piggyback on our first set of heads, we could record entirely different information (signal) on the bottom half of the tape. In fact, this is how our stereo tape recorders are made, i.e. with a "stacked" (double) set of erase, record and playback heads. Each set of heads has its independent set of electronics—record amplifiers for the record heads and playback amplifiers for the playback heads. The purpose of this is not to save tape, but to be able to record different information on each track simultaneously. Usually in stereo recording we record the left track of information on one track and the right track on the other.

Of course, since there is a completely separate set of heads and electronics, we could record on one track at a time with completely different information on each track. Normally, we use ¼" tape for two-track recording. But suppose we wish to increase the head stack to four separate heads, one on top of the other. We could then record or play back four separate channels of information, either one at a time or all together or in whatever combination that we want. For best results, we would now use a tape ½" wide. Carrying the same idea forward, we could stack any number of heads together. Most recording studios now have at least an 8-track machine, and many have 16-track facilities.

Most recordings made today take advantage of multi-track recording techniques. For example, in doing a rock recording we would first probably record just rhythm tracks. On track #1 we would record bass drum, track #2 snare drum, track #3 tom-toms, and track #4 cymbals. We might record the electric bass on track #5 and rhythm guitar on track #6, with possible tambourine or special rhythm instruments on track #7. At the next recording session at a later time, we could record the lead guitar on track #8. Then the lead vocal would go onto track #9, and since we might want a choice of interpretations, we might use tracks #10 and #11 as alternate vocals. Then the back-up vocal parts would be recorded on tracks #12, #13 and #14. This could all be done over a period of time, one track at a time. Up to this point the job for the recording engineer has been made simple, while the musicians' job has been harder. They have had to listen to the previously recorded tracks through earphones while playing along. But now the engineer has to take the recorded tracks and mix them together at varying levels to get a good musical balance, and the resultant mix is usually re-recorded on a two-track (stereo) tape recorder.

E. Sel-Sync

In order to be able to play back previously recorded tracks while recording additional tracks, as in the prior example, it is necessary to play the pre-recorded tracks back, not on the playback head, but from the record head. The reason for this is quite simple. If we were to listen to the playback head, and record our new tracks with this, the new tracks would not be synchronized with the old. This is because of the time that it takes for one point on the tape to travel between the record head and the playback head a few inches away. Since the construction of the record head is similar to the playback head, we can simply use the record head as a playback head so that the new tracks will be synchronized with the previously recorded tracks. This over-recording process is called *sel-sync*, or *overdubbing* (Figure 15).

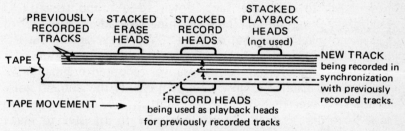

On a multi-track tape recorder we use sel-syncing to synchronise a new track being recorded with previously recorded tracks. To do this we use sections of the record head as playback heads in order to play back the previously recorded tracks at the same place on the tape that we are recording.

FIGURE 15

F. Signal-to-Noise Ratio

A certain amount of *ambient noise* (background noise) exists in any audio system. This ambient noise exists outside of the recording studio, too, in real life. Suppose that you leave your apartment in the morning and meet a friend in the elevator. You start a conversation and don't have to speak too loudly to be heard since the only ambient noise is the elevator mechanism. As you walk out of the building there is heavy street traffic, so you have to speak louder in order to be heard. As you walk you pass a street repair crew using pneumatic hammers to break up the street. The ambient noise level is now so high that you have to shout to be heard. The signal (your voice) and the noise (ambient sound not related to the signal) can be compared by a ratio expressed in decibels. Because of the nature of electronic components and the noise that is generated as tape passes over a playback head, there is always some ambient noise in the studio. Naturally, we try to keep this as low as possible through proper design and maintenance of equipment. When we say that the signal-to-noise ratio is "65 db," we mean that when the signal we are recording is at "0 db," the ambient noise is 65 db below the signal.

G. "Generations"

Suppose that we have made a recording on our 16-track tape recorder and we have kept the signal-to-noise ratio at -55 db. We now have to mix the tape down to a mono (one-track) recording, using another tape machine. We adjust the level of the mono machine so that we get a "0" level average on our VU meter. However, it is not just signal that we are recording; it is signal plus whatever ambient noise was recorded originally. We finish the transfer, but now we have not only the ambient noise of the first tape recorder, but the ambient noise of the second tape recorder as well. As we continue to transfer to make additional copies, we continue to add ambient noise until eventually, the noise could be louder than the signal. Each succeeding transfer is called a generation and they are numbered "first generation," "second generation," etc. With each succeeding generation, there is a deterioration of quality. Often, we do have to go to five or six generations. For example, suppose that the tape made above is for a film background score. We now have a first-generation mix-down of our 16-track (abbreviated 16X) original tape, on ¼" mono tape. It must now be transferred to 16 or 35 millimeter magnetic film. This looks like regular sprocketed motion picture film except that it has a magnetic coating on it and it can be recorded on just like a regular tape recorder. This is used because it can be edited and cut against the actual film. It is now a second-generation tape. Eventually, a sound mix of the film is done. The music on magnetic film must be mixed with the voice which may be on another piece of magnetic film, and the sound effects which are on additional pieces of film. These are combined against the picture and recorded on still another piece of magnetic film.

This is our third generation.

The mixed sound track (on magnetic film) now has to be converted to an optical track, where our signal activates a magnet which opens and closes an iris to change the exposure on photographic film. This becomes our fourth generation. Now, additional circulation prints of the film have to be made so that the final sound the audience hears is five or more generations away from the original. If the signal-to-noise ratio is not kept at a minimum in each step, you will end up with a very noisy sound track. Various types of filtering and equalization systems are used to help minimize the noise levels, but they, in turn, introduce distortion and other problems. It is better to cure the disease early in the game before it has time to develop (Figure 16).

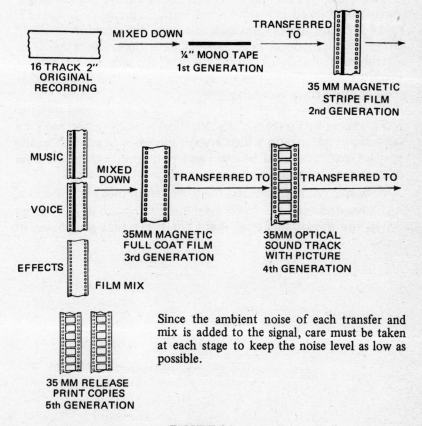

MIXED DOWN

TRANSFERRED TO

16 TRACK 2"
ORIGINAL
RECORDING

¼" MONO TAPE
1st GENERATION

35 MM MAGNETIC
STRIPE FILM
2nd GENERATION

MUSIC

VOICE

EFFECTS

MIXED DOWN

TRANSFERRED TO

TRANSFERRED TO

35MM MAGNETIC
FULL COAT FILM
3rd GENERATION

35MM OPTICAL
SOUND TRACK
WITH PICTURE
4th GENERATION

FILM MIX

Since the ambient noise of each transfer and mix is added to the signal, care must be taken at each stage to keep the noise level as low as possible.

35 MM RELEASE
PRINT COPIES
5th GENERATION

FIGURE 16

Summary

The most common method of sound recording today is with the magnetic tape recorder, which records on a plastic tape bonded to a magnetic metal oxide. The tape recorder is a device which provides an even movement of tape past a series of coils and electromagnets which induce onto the tape coating varying degrees of magnetism in step with the audio signal. In turn, when a magnetized piece of tape is drawn past a coil of wire, the varying magnetic fluctuations induce an alternating current in the coil of wire in direct ratio to the changes in the magnetic flux. The tape recorder also supplies the mechanism to wind tape on reels at various speeds, forward as well as reverse. The tape recorder also provides the electronics to amplify signal levels as well as to meter them.

The erase, record and playback coils can be set up singly (mono) or stacked in various combinations, giving us 2, 4, 8, 12 or 16 separate tracks on which to record different information, either simultaneously or one track at a time. Sometimes, to synchronize tracks, we want to use the record head as a playback head. This is called sel-sync, or overdubbing, and is used in multi-track recording.

Ambient noise level can be expressed as a signal-to-noise ratio, and as we go from one generation to the next we record a cumulative noise ratio which always increases in relation to the signal. Great care must be exercised to minimize the noise level of each piece of equipment used.

Now that we have covered the basic terminology of acoustics, and have discussed the basic machinery of recording, we can go on to the use of this equipment for the actual generation of music.

4. Some Classical Tape Recorder Electronic Music Techniques

A. Tape Speed and Pitch

The speed at which tape passes the playback head has a direct effect on the pitch of the sound. If we record an "A" at 440 Hz. at a speed of 7½ IPS and then play the tape back at double speed, 15 IPS, the pitch will also be double, or 880 Hz. Therefore, if we were to record a tuba at a very low speed and then play back the tape at four times the speed, we would have a tuba playing four octaves higher (and four times as fast in tempo). The whole harmonic spectrum would also be shifted, and in effect, we would have a new instrument sounding quite different from a tuba. Naturally, any rhythmic pattern that we record will vary in direct ratio to the speed of the tape. Compositionally, this can be a very useful technique.

B. Tape Direction and the Envelope

A recorded sound can be greatly altered if we reverse the direction in which the tape passes the playback head. The envelope (loudness pattern) will be reversed, and we can completely change a sound by using this technique. On instruments with a set attack pattern, this can be most effective. For example, a piano tone played backward will have the snap of the attack at the end of the sound with a swell up to it. The human voice, singing or speaking, when played backward, sounds like some strange other-worldly language.

C. Splicing Techniques

By recording different sounds and editing the tape so that the different sounds occur in some sort of a sequence, interesting effects can be achieved. Splicing techniques present a wide range of possibilities. By sequencing various sounds, musical compositions can be made from separate sound sources organized from bits and pieces of tape. For rests (silence), either blank tape or *leader tape* can be used. Leader tape is simply paper tape with no magnetic coating. As this passes the playback head there will be silence. These techniques, which are the earliest tape recorder techniques, are best done on a mono tape recorder since there is no way in which a single track can be edited out of an 8-track tape. However, we can record what we want on a mono tape and then transfer it onto an 8- or 16-track tape and build up each track, layer by layer, just as we would work with live instruments.

Generally, tape recorder techniques for the generation of musical composition take a great deal of pre-planning, patience and splicing tape. Tape manipulation can provide us with many interesting sounds, but to organize them into a musically valid idea requires real talent.

Summary

Pre-recorded sounds can be altered through the use of the tape recorder itself. The pitch of the fundamental tone as well as the harmonic spectrum can be raised or lowered in direct ratio to the speed at which the tape is drawn past the playback head. Therefore, one octave of pitch change will occur when we double or halve the tape speed. Reversing the movement of the tape past the playback head will reverse the envelope (loudness pattern) of a sound, and by splicing various pre-recorded sounds together we can create a sequence of separate sounds and tones.

5. The Electronic Music Synthesizer

A. General Description of All Musical Instruments

The first instrument man used for the organization of coherent sound into a form of expression and communication was, of course, the human voice. This has continued to be the ideal instrument throughout the ages. Other instruments were developed from devices originally intended for nonmusical purposes. Used for signaling, they were generally of the percussive type, which could be heard for a greater distance than the voice.

Acoustical instruments continued to develop artistically, but they were used either to accompany or to augment the human voice in some way. Until the late Middle Ages, instrumental music as we know it was rare. As the leisure arts developed during the Renaissance, instruments and instrumental music advanced further, but still to a great extent as an auxiliary to vocal music.

Ideally then, the instruments most capable of human emotion and expression are those which can best emulate characteristics of the human voice, as follows:

dynamic range from very soft to very loud

infinite pitch resolution, i.e. the ability to produce any frequency within its range, either in discrete movement or gliding through all intermediate frequencies

variation of timbre over a wide range at will

variable duration, i.e. control of the length of time that a tone may be sustained with infinite variations in amplitude.

Those western acoustical instruments which are considered the most expressive, such as the violin, have these characteristics of the human voice.

B. General Description of Electronic Musical Instruments Other than Synthesizers

Electronic organs have existed since the early 1930's, in many different shapes, forms and variations. The *Hammond Organ,* one of the most widely known, uses an electro-mechanical system to generate its sound. Faceted magnetized discs are rotated near coils of wire to generate an alternating electric current. A pure sine wave is formed which passes through a series of switches called *stops* and *pull tabs* and is combined with other related sine waves in the overtone series to form more complex wave patterns (Figure 17).

Most other electronic organs, as we learned earlier, consist of a series of oscillators which are built to produce a very stable fixed pitch, one oscillator for each of the 12 highest tones of the keyboard. For each successively lower octave of these 12 tones, an electronic circuit divides the frequency in half. These instruments are often called *divider organs,* since all lower octave notes are created by dividing the frequencies of the highest 12 master oscillators. Stops and tabs are used, but rather

HAMMOND ORGAN TONE WHEEL PITCH GENERATOR

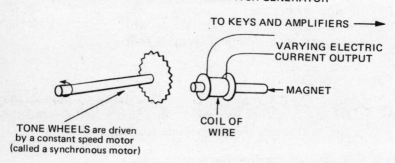

A faceted steel disc is rotated by a constant speed motor. A magnet with a coil of wire around it is placed near the tone wheel. As the "teeth" on the steel disc pass by the magnet, a varying electric current is induced into the coil of wire. The speed at which the steel disc rotates, as well as the number of teeth on the disc, determines the frequency (pitch) of the varying electric current.

FIGURE 17

than synthesize more complex tones by combining sine waves, as in the case of the Hammond Organ, the oscillators are built to produce a complex wave form to begin with, and filters are then used to modify the tone colors by removing some of the harmonics.

In comparison with the human voice, we find a number of shortcomings. The most obvious are (1) only discrete pitches are possible; there is no way to produce a true glissando; (2) variations of tone color on a sustained note is at best cumbersome; and (3) basically, the loudness pattern is fixed, i.e. the note is either on or off. The *swell pedal* can change the dynamic level, but without the subtlety of the human voice. Of course, the organ has many unique and desirable features of its own. We are only comparing those features it has in common with the human voice.

C. General Description of the Electronic Music Synthesizer

The most important factor which sets the electronic music synthesizer apart from the other electronic instruments is that the oscillators on a synthesizer are *variable pitch oscillators*. They can be made to change their frequency from a sub-audible tone (below 25 Hz.) to the highest pitches that we can hear. This overcomes the inadequacies of the fixed-pitch organ oscillators so that the synthesizer can glide between all the frequencies between two fixed pitches as the human voice does. The synthesizer tends to be used as a *monophonic* (one note sounding at a time) instrument. More complex polyphonic keyboards (where chords can be played) have been built, but they are quite rare. Some synthesizers are now being made with a two-note capability, i.e. the highest and lowest keys depressed will each control their own independent oscillators.

On the synthesizer, the filters which are used to modify the tone color are also variable and can change the timbre of the tone as it is sounding, very much as the human voice does. The amplifiers on the synthesizer are also variable so that the loudness and duration pattern can be varied over a wide range.

Therefore, a synthesizer may be said to compare very favorably with the human voice as far as the criteria we have established are concerned: (1) it has infinite resolution and range of pitch; (2) it has a wide range of timbre control; (3) it has infinite duration control from the shortest discernible sound to one infinitely long; and (4) it has a wide dynamic (loudness) range.

D. Some Capabilities of the Synthesizer Beyond the Human Voice and Acoustical Instruments

The electronic music synthesizer opens up a whole new world of sounds which are completely new and distinct. For example, we have seen that the range of frequencies and the speed at which they can be varied is much greater than any other instrument. This can give the composer a flexibility never before available, because the variable pitch oscillators of the synthesizer can jump from the lowest audible pitch to the highest almost instantaneously.

All previous acoustical and electronic instruments generated their tone colors by varying the balance between a given pitch and various harmonics in a related overtone series. On the synthesizer we can tune a series of oscillators into a relationship not related to the overtone series. In effect, we can invent our own harmonic overtone series using any frequencies that we desire. This makes it possible to generate tens of thousands of entirely new sounds, an area for great explorations.

The synthesizer keyboard can be tuned with infinite variation. Instead of the traditional semitone tuning, we can program the keyboard so that two adjacent keys can initiate the sound of an interval of less than a semitone (microtonal) or more than a semitone (macrotonal). This, too, is an area for great discoveries.

One oscillator may be used to modify the sound of another oscillator so that the pitch of the second oscillator changes in a regular periodic manner. This is called *frequency modulation*. Many new and useful sounds are created in this manner.

An oscillator may also be used to change the band pass and frequency response of a filter, which produces some remarkable effects.

Since the synthesizer is so new, we have only just begun to explore the areas of sound fabrication (Figure 18).

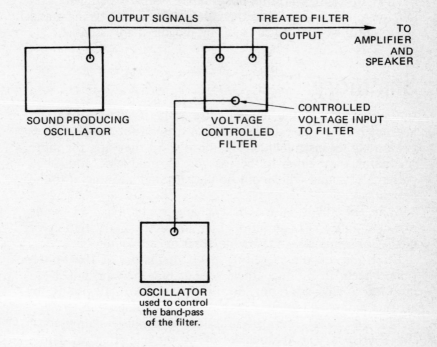

OUTPUT SIGNALS — TREATED FILTER OUTPUT — TO AMPLIFIER AND SPEAKER

SOUND PRODUCING OSCILLATOR

VOLTAGE CONTROLLED FILTER

CONTROLLED VOLTAGE INPUT TO FILTER

OSCILLATOR
used to control
the band-pass
of the filter.

An Oscillator can be used both as a signal source and as a source of controlling voltage for a filter, an amplifier or another oscillator.

FIGURE 18

E. Programming the Synthesizer

Synthesizers are comprised of a number of basic sections which we will examine in detail later. These sections consist of sound producers, filters, amplifiers, mixers, and a series of voltage-regulating elements, e.g. keyboard, touch plate, foot pedal, joy stick, etc.

These sections may be interconnected in tens of thousands of different ways. We use the term *programming* to describe which of the various sections will be used and how they will be interconnected. Obviously, a knowledge of the synthesizer is essential, as well as a knowledge of music, since the manner in which the sections are interconnected determines what sound will be created. It is like inventing a new instrument every time the synthesizer is programmed. Because of the tremendous number of interconnecting possibilities, much experimentation has to be done. Just as in the case of the skilled arranger and orchestrator, good musical taste and judgment are essential.

Summary

If we assume that the human voice is the most nearly perfect instrument, we can establish certain criteria for the characteristics of other instruments. The more vocal they are, the more successful they tend to be, as far as producing controlled patterns of sound which will be pleasing and meaningful to the human ear.

Some of these basic vocal characteristics are: (1) wide dynamic range, (2) infinite pitch variation, (3) variation of quality of sound and (4) variable duration and loudness.

Electronic organs use either fixed oscillators or fixed-pitch tone wheels to produce their sound, but they are unable to produce a glissando; nor do they have great flexibility in altering timbre and loudness as a tone is sounding.

The electronic music synthesizer does have many vocal characteristics. The frequencies of its variable-pitch oscillators can be varied infinitely. Tone colors and dynamic range can be changed over a wide latitude.

The synthesizer can also generate many sounds which cannot be produced by the human voice, nor by any other instrument. Great flexibility in the control of the movement of pitches is available to the composer. Modifications by oscillators to produce various forms of modulation can be used to produce whole new areas of sound.

The interconnecting of various sections of the synthesizer is called programming. The possible ways of interconnecting the sound producers, filters, amplifiers, mixers and voltage-regulators number into the tens of thousands. Each new interconnection produces a different sound.

The programmer must be a combination orchestrator and instrument builder, since, in effect, he is designing a new musical instrument each time he changes the interconnections.

Since the synthesizer does have many of the elements of the human voice, its validity as a musical instrument is assured. If it is used with good musical taste, it can open entirely new facets of sound to the composer and listener.

6. Using Electronic Music Synthesizers

A. Modular and Nonmodular Instruments

The synthesizer may either be made up of a series of separate and independent *modules* (sections) or all of the different sections may be mounted on one frame. The advantage of modular construction is that each separate section can be unplugged and removed without disabling the rest of the instrument. For servicing, this is quite useful. Besides, there is an advantage in the greater facility with which additional modules may be added. The disadvantages are an increase in weight and in the cost of manufacturing. However, many nonmodular units have the various electronic circuits built on separate electronic circuit boards which can be unplugged for servicing.

B. The Power Supply

All synthesizers must have a power supply which takes line current, whose voltage fluctuates depending on the power company and whatever else is on the line, and converts it into a very steady direct current (DC) voltage. It is important that this be very carefully designed so that no matter how the AC line voltage varies, it will produce a constant DC voltage. There is one alternative, which is to use batteries. The power supply is controlled by an on-off switch which generally turns on the entire synthesizer. There is usually a fuse system. A *fuse* is a "weak link" which is designed to burn out first before a more expensive component burns out due to a malfunction. The rating of the fuse is clearly marked; if it needs replacing, it should always be with a fuse of the same recommended size.

C. Voltage Control

The key to the design of most synthesizers is the element of *voltage control*. When we discussed oscillators, filters and amplifiers, we found that their functions were dependent on the power provided by some external source. If we change the controlling voltage to an oscillator, the speed at which it oscillates will change. If we change the controlling voltage to a filter, the band pass will change; and if we change the controlling voltage to an amplifier, the amplification factor will change. All true synthesizers depend on voltage control to direct the function of each section: oscillators, filters and amplifiers. Voltage control is the invisible hand which, in effect, changes the knob setting on each of the synthesizer components.

D. Voltage Controlled Oscillators

The true "heart" of the synthesizer is the *voltage-controlled oscillator*. This is the primary sound source, so it is important to understand its construction. The quality and design of the oscillator are most important, because the stability of the oscillator and its ability to "track" (keep in tune) with other oscillators though its entire range are critical. These oscillators are designed so that there is a relationship between the controlling voltage and the frequency output. The higher the control voltage, the higher the pitch. Generally, this relationship is such that, for each volt added as a control voltage, the oscillators will double their frequency, i.e. sound an octave higher.

There are basic tuning controls on the front panel of all oscillators. A switch is usually used to set the basic range, either low pitch and high pitch; or a "stepped" switch (multi-position switch) is provided which will switch the basic frequency by octaves. Sometimes this is marked with organ pipe designations, e.g. 4′, 8′, 16′ and 32′. A "low" position may also be provided. This produces a *sub-audible* tone whose frequency is so low (generally below 25 Hz.) that we tend to hear it as a series of pops, like a gasoline lawn mower engine. There is also a *vernier control knob* named after Pierre Vernier (1580-1633). This provides a continuous voltage to the oscillator so that it can be finely tuned between the steps of the octave, or high-low, switch. Therefore, these are the two main controls for setting the basic frequency of our voltage-controlled oscillators: a coarse tuning, either by octave or simply a "high-low" switch, and a vernier to give us fine tuning of the pitch. Sometimes a third switch is provided for a second coarse-tuning option.

The output of most oscillators is a series of different wave shapes. These are selectable either by switch, pin matrix, or output jack. We will explain the various methods used to interconnect sections later.

The basic wave shape output is a *sine wave.* In fact, all of the more complex wave shapes are a compounding of the basic sine wave, at different frequencies and at various amplitudes. The sine wave is a very pure wave shape in that it has no overtones at all. It is pure fundamental, and its shape is very much like the waves in a pond. It produces a non-piercing mellow sound, like the pure sound of a flute. On an oscilloscope, it would look like this:

~~~.This sign is used to designate the output on some synthesizers, while others simply say "sine."

The second output choice from the oscillator is a modified sine wave which has some harmonics present. This is called a *triangle wave.* On an oscilloscope it would look like this:

∧∧∧ .This sound has the characteristic of a clarinet in the lowest register. It is rather reedy, but not piercing.

The third output choice is a *sawtooth wave.* This is rich in all harmonics and is quite a strong piercing sound. If we look at this waveshape on our oscilloscope, it would look like the teeth of a saw: ∕⊿⊿⊿ . It can be reversed to look like this: ⊾⊿⊿⊾ , but the sound is the same. The reversed sawtooth is sometimes called a *ramp wave.*

The fourth output choice is called a *square wave.* It is very rich in a different series of harmonics from the sawtooth wave and therefore has a different sound, much like a harsher clarinet. On an oscilloscope it would look like this: ⊓⊔⊓⊔ .

Because of the on-off characteristics of a square wave (it is either up or down and therefore has switch characteristics), it could also be called a *pulse wave,* since it pulses up and down. We can alter this pulse wave shape so that it can be up for a longer period than down, in a varying ratio, like this: ⊓⊔⊓⊔⊓ . On some synthesizers two or three different pulse widths are available. On others, the pulse width is continuously variable by means of a control knob marked "width of pulse." The varying width of a pulse wave is called the *duty cycle.* The actual sound varies from a harsh clarinet sound of the square wave to a still harsher sound, with a lot of higher-frequency harmonics. By spending some time listening to the various tonal colors that are available you can become familiar with the distinctive sounds of the various wave shapes. Unfortunately, we must use either technical designations for the various wave shapes or pictures of them, because no musical description exists.

On some synthesizers, the various wave-shape outputs have their own volume control, so that the level of the wave shape can be controlled as it leaves the oscillator.

All synthesizer oscillators must also have some way for injecting the controlling voltage. As you will recall, this is the voltage which tells the oscillator at what frequency to function. There may be one or more *voltage control inputs* to the oscillator, since we sometimes want to use more than one control voltage to give directions to the oscillator at the same time. These various voltage control inputs are combined additively in a *summing network,* a system for algebraically adding the various control voltages together. We say "algebraically" because we might be adding a positive voltage to a negative voltage. If one control voltage is plus 4 volts and it is added to a voltage that may be minus 6 volts, the summing circuit will give a minus 2 volt output (Figure 19).

When a series of independent modules (or units) are combined to function in parallel, it is called *ganging.* The ganging of oscillators is quite common, and on most synthesizers a system is provided to gang a series of oscillators. This simply means that with the front panel high-low range, octave and vernier controls, we can tune a series of oscillators, let us say, for example, as follows: the first a fundamental, the second at an octave, the third at a twelfth, and so on. Now, if we can use the same control voltage to control the varying frequencies of all the oscillators, then they will move in step, maintaining the same intervalic relationship to each other that we set up initially. The design of each oscillator is quite critical, since they all must change frequency exactly in step. One of the main advantages of a synthesizer over a conventional electronic organ is in this programming capability. Most conventional instruments achieve their tonal color, as we have explained, by generating a spectrum of harmonics, all of which are related to the fundamental tone in the ratio of small whole numbers. These will be in various strengths (amplitudes), but always an octave, a twelfth, a double octave, a third above this, a fifth, a dominant seventh, a triple octave, etc. On a synthesizer, we can tune our oscillators to this same pattern and in some ways re-create the sound of conventional instruments. This, of course, is not the true purpose of a synthesizer any more than the true purpose of an organ stop is to create an orchestral instrument sound. However, on a synthesizer, since the oscillators are infinitely tunable, we can tune them so that the harmonics heard from the higher oscillators are not in the ratio of small whole numbers and a completely unique. harmonic spectrum can be generated that is unlike any conventional instrument. It is an area for much experimentation, because each new combination of available oscillators is a determining factor as to how complex a sound we can construct (Figure 20).

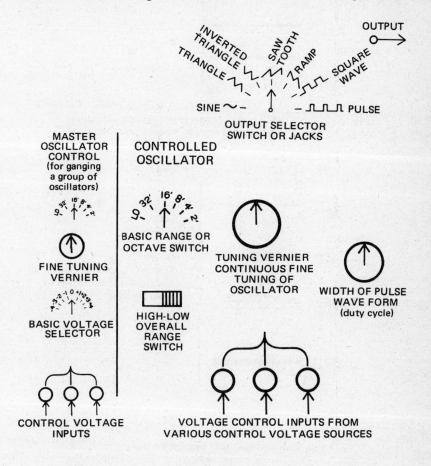

Basic controls and functions of a voltage-controlled Oscillator.

FIGURE 19

CONVENTIONAL INSTRUMENT OVERTONE SYSTEM

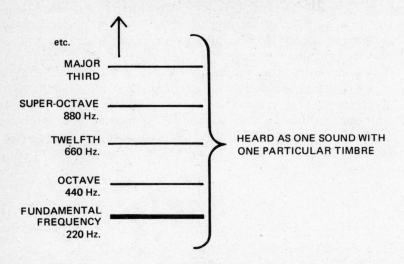

etc.

MAJOR
THIRD

SUPER-OCTAVE
880 Hz.

TWELFTH   HEARD AS ONE SOUND WITH
660 Hz.   ONE PARTICULAR TIMBRE

OCTAVE
440 Hz.

FUNDAMENTAL
FREQUENCY
220 Hz.

**UNLIMITED SYNTHESIZER POSSIBILITIES USING A SERIES
OF OSCILLATORS TUNED TO NON-REGULAR HARMONICS**

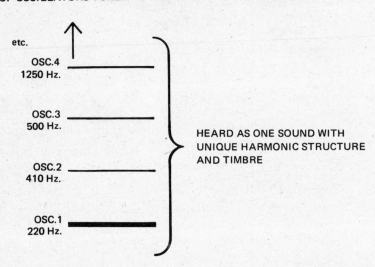

etc.

OSC.4
1250 Hz.

OSC.3
500 Hz.

HEARD AS ONE SOUND WITH
OSC.2   UNIQUE HARMONIC STRUCTURE
410 Hz.   AND TIMBRE

OSC.1
220 Hz.

With conventional instruments, the harmonics occur in the ratio of small, whole numbers. With a synthesizer we can create an overtone series in any ratio that we desire by ganging and tuning a series of voltage-controlled oscillators.

FIGURE 20

E. White and Pink Sound

As you may recall, *white noise* was described as all audible frequencies sounding randomly at random amplitudes. White noise sounds like a roar and hiss combined. If you tune to a blank channel on your television, you will hear a roar similar to pure white noise. *Pink noise* is similar to white noise except that the lower frequencies are weighted to sound a little louder than the upper frequencies.

All synthesizers provide a white noise and often a pink noise supply. This is the second sound source on a synthesizer, and the unit is supplied with an output connection, a switch to select white or pink noise, and sometimes a volume control. It is important to remember that on most synthesizers, both the oscillators and white sound source are producing signals at all times. If you do not connect this signal to an amplifier and speaker, it will not be heard, but it is functioning at all times.

F. External Signal Input

A third signal input can come from an *external source*. Most synthesizers make provision for a microphone or low-level signal input. This input usually has to be amplified, so there is a special amplifier to bring it up to what is needed as a signal level in the sections of the synthesizer. This external signal can be a microphone or a direct input from an electronic instrument, such as an electric guitar or electric piano. This signal can then be modified by the filters and amplifiers in the synthesizer, as well as being combined with or modified by the internal sound sources (oscillator and white noise) of the synthesizer.

Therefore, the three basic sound sources in a synthesizer are oscillators, white-pink noise generators, and external signal source.

G. Fixed and Variable Filters

Most synthesizers provide two basic types of filters: a *fixed filter,* which allows predetermined frequencies to pass; and a *variable voltage-controlled filter,* whose band pass of frequencies is governed by controlling voltage.

The passive filter can be a step switch filter, where each step of a multi-position switch will give an increasingly higher band pass (a low pass filter), or the converse, where each step of the switch cuts out the lower frequencies by degrees (a high pass filter). Some filters replace the step switch with a continuously variable filtering system very much like the tone controls on a hi-fi. A high pass filter will increase the ratio of high frequencies to low, and a low pass will increase the ratio of low frequencies to high.

A more sophisticated version of this filter has a separate boost control for a great number of separate bands of frequencies. This is usually broken down into half or third octaves, and each narrow band of frequencies can be boosted or attenuated (lessened). This type of filter is called an *equalizer*, since it can be used to balance (or equalize) a signal by changing the relative dynamic level between a fundamental tone and its various harmonics.

The *voltage-controlled filters* can be divided into two classes: low and high pass. On some synthesizers both high and low pass signal can be recovered from the same unit; on others separate units are used. The band that these filters will pass is determined by a control voltage. As voltage is applied to a low pass filter, it will pass the fundamental of a complex signal, and then, as more voltage is supplied as a control, the various higher harmonics will be added, in ascending order. An "emphasis," "regeneration" or "resonance" control is usually provided, which balances the amplitude of the higher frequencies in relationship to the lower. With this control turned full on, the filter itself will usually go into oscillation. On a voltage-controlled high pass filter, as control voltage increases, the lower frequencies of a complex sound are diminished until they disappear, leaving only the higher harmonics audible.

Generally, there is a control knob on these filters which provides an initial control voltage to the filter, and which sets its band pass. If this voltage sets the band pass below the frequency of the input signal, nothing will be heard. There must always be a signal input to the filter from a signal-generating source (oscillator, white-pink generator or external signal), and there must always be an output where the treated signal leaves the filter. Sometimes there is an additional stepped *range switch* which works in conjunction with the control knob that sets the initial band pass of the filter, thus increasing its range.

There is always an additional input connection for a *control voltage input*. In fact, there are usually a group of these inputs so that a combination of control voltage may be applied. They are summed as on the oscillators (Figure 21).

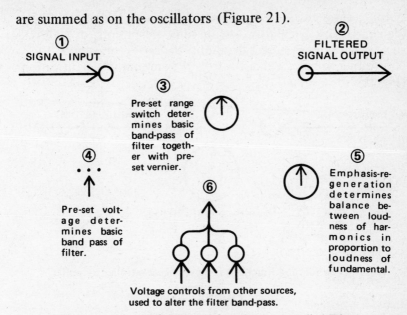

Basic controls and functions of a voltage-controlled Filter.

FIGURE 21

A *filter coupler* is available on some synthesizers in order to couple the functions of the high and low pass filters so that they will work in tandem. The coupler is also voltage controlled and has a mode switch to select whether the filters work as band pass or as band reject filters. The center frequency is voltage-controllable, as are the width of frequencies the filter will pass.

H. Voltage–Controlled Amplifiers

The third major section of the synthesizer consists of *voltage-controlled amplifiers*. As you recall, an amplifier is a device which takes an alternating current signal and makes it louder. A voltage-controlled amplifier will amplify in proportion to the control voltage that is applied; the greater the control voltage, the louder the output signal. If no control voltage is applied, the amplifier will not pass any signal at all. There is a manual gain control which can be used to set the level of the signal passing through the amplifier. This knob supplies a fixed control voltage to the amplifier. There is a signal input and a signal output through which a path is provided for the signal (generated by oscillators, white-pink generators or external signals). There is also an input or series of inputs for a controlling voltage, which controls the amount of amplification (Figure 22).

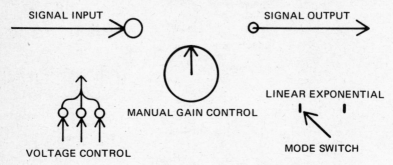

Basic controls and functions for a voltage-controlled amplifier.

FIGURE 22

These amplifiers are generally built so that they have two amplifying functions, selected by a mode switch. The two functions are *linear amplification* and *exponential amplification*. Linear (a straight line) amplification means that for a level of loudness with one volt of control voltage, at two volts the sound level will be twice as loud. At three volts, it will be three times as loud, etc. Exponential amplification means that the amplifier will not only increase the amplitude, but it does so at an increasing rate. A sound level at one volt will be not merely twice as loud at two volts, but perhaps 2½ times as loud. At three volts, it may be five times as loud, etc. (Figure 23).

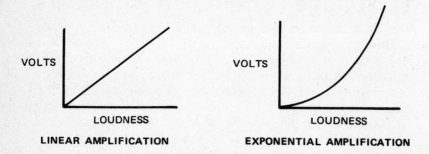

FIGURE 23

Summary

The synthesizer can be constructed with each function built as a separate module or the entire synthesizer can be built on one plate. A power supply takes regular line current and converts it into a very constant DC voltage. There are three main sections to a synthesizer: (1) the sound-generating source, (2) the filtering system and (3) the amplifying section. There are three basic sources of sound: (1) oscillators, (2) white-pink noise generators and (3) an external signal source.

These signals can then be treated by filters. A fixed filter passes preset frequencies and rejects all others. A voltage-controlled filter uses a control voltage to determine which frequency bands it will pass. Voltage-controlled filters are generally divided into high pass filters which tend to pass high frequencies and reject low frequencies, and low pass filters, which pass low frequencies and reject highs.

The amplifying system consists of an amplifier whose gain is determined by a control voltage; the higher the voltage, the greater the gain. It can amplify in a linear or exponential mode.

7. Voltage Control Sources

A. Introduction

We have seen that the three main sections of the synthesizer are voltage-controlled oscillators, voltage-controlled filters and voltage-controlled amplifiers. We must have a number of controlling sources to provide us with these controlling voltages, for it is by their direction that each section knows what to do.

B. The Keyboard

One of the commonest sources of control voltage is the *keyboard switching device*. Since the keyboard is universally known to musicians, it provides a good interface (interconnection between unlike systems) between the instrument and the musician. Normally, a standard 3- to 6-octave commercial organ keyboard is used, and the switch contact under each key provides a means of switching in various voltage levels. The oscillators are usually designed so that they double frequency (go up an octave) for each control voltage increase of one volt. Therefore, to get the 12 semitones that we need for a chromatic octave, each ascending key must provide one-twelfth of a volt more than the key below it. This will provide us with a *tempered octave* where each semitone is exactly equidistant from the next. Some keyboards are provided with an external programming device consisting of a separate tuning control for each keyboard key. There is a separate selector switch for external tuning if you want to tune a nontempered scale.

Since we are getting a selectable DC voltage from the keyboard, this can be connected as a control voltage to an oscillator to give us pitch changes, or to a filter control voltage input to give us different band pass characteristics, or to an amplifier to control the loudness of a signal. And since this is a DC control voltage, we can attenuate it with a *potentiometer* (a volume control knob) so that for every physical octave on the keyboard, the oscillator can be made to receive less than the one volt it needs to double frequency. This means that all types of *microtonal* scales can be set up. A microtonal scale is a scale where smaller divisions than a semitone are used. Normally, we have 12 semitones to an octave, but now it is possible to program a quarter tone, eighth tone or any other division that we want. We can also increase the output voltage of the keyboard so that we can produce *macrotonal scales,* scales where the smallest division is more than a semitone. This has never been achieved easily on other instruments, but with the synthesizer much experimentation can readily be done. The typical keyboard is provided with an over-all *tuning control* which will transpose the keyboard. We must be sure that "A"−440 Hz.−is where we want it, since the physical "A" key can be tuned to produce any frequency we want.

There is usually a *scale adjustment* control on the keyboard which will fine tune the octaves. Since octaves can be made wider or narrower, the keyboard should be adjusted if you want a tempered scale, so that the octaves are exactly double the frequency of the octave below.

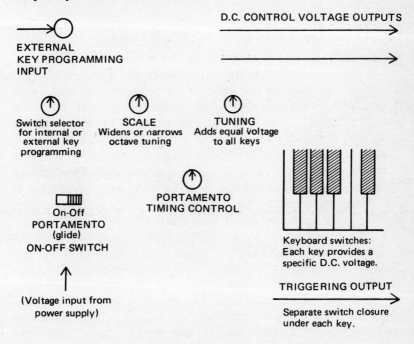

Basic controls of a Keyboard voltage source.

FIGURE 24

The *portamento* or *glide* switch turns on a circuit which allows the voltage to change gradually between one key and another, giving a sliding effect instead of a discrete (immediate) pitch change from one key to another. There is a *portamento control* which sets the time that it will take for the sounding note to move from one pitch completely to the next when a new key is depressed.

A *power supply connection* is provided to supply the keyboard with its voltage; of course, the keyboard itself does not produce any sound; it simply supplies a control voltage which is key-variable. On some keyboards, more than one key can be used at a time, giving two or more separate control voltage outputs. These can be used to control two independent banks of oscillators or for any other voltage-control function. Normally, the lower key, when depressed, will disable any higher keys depressed. An additional switch is provided under each key to provide a *triggering function* which we will describe in the next section (Figure 24).

C. The Envelope Generator

An *envelope generator* is a timing device which gives a timed rise in voltage, a timed decrease in voltage and a sustain voltage. All three can be used for controlling voltage-controlled oscillators, filters and amplifiers. A series of control knobs is provided to set each function. Sometimes these knobs are calibrated in actual time values of milliseconds (thousandths of a second) and seconds.

The first control knob is a *rise time* voltage. This give an increasing DC control voltage over the time span for which it is set. When it completes the time for which it is set, the control voltage is at a maximum. It then shuts itself off and turns on the next function.

The second control knob begins to work as soon as the rise time voltage cycle is complete. This is the *initial decay* function. It gives a decreasing voltage output for the time to which it is set, and then turns itself off. The rise time and initial decay time function can be used together or separately. If the rise time function is not needed, we simply zero (turn full counter clockwise) the control knob. The decay function will begin immediately.

Should we not want the initial decay function to return all of the way to zero volts, we have a third control, usually called *sustain*. We can set this so that, as the voltage decreases from the initial decay function, it will drop only until it gets to the level set by the sustain control.

A final control knob controls the *final decay* which occurs after the sustain function.

The envelope generator must know when to begin generating its voltages. Therefore a provision is made for *triggering* (also called *gating*). The extra set of key switches mentioned in the section on keyboard controllers are used to trigger the envelope generator; it puts out a control voltage in accordance with how it is set. It will finish its timed cycle unless it is retriggered in the middle of a cycle. If this occurs, it will start its function from the beginning again. This timed voltage output can be used to control oscillators and filters, but most often amplifiers. It must have a triggering input and a control voltage output (Figure 25).

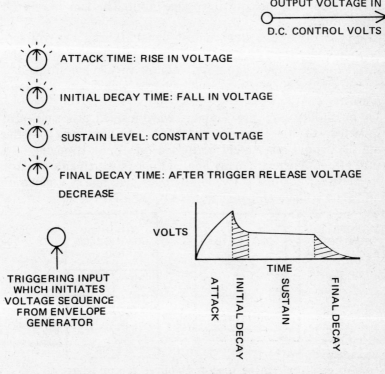

OUTPUT VOLTAGE IN

D.C. CONTROL VOLTS

ATTACK TIME: RISE IN VOLTAGE

INITIAL DECAY TIME: FALL IN VOLTAGE

SUSTAIN LEVEL: CONSTANT VOLTAGE

FINAL DECAY TIME: AFTER TRIGGER RELEASE VOLTAGE DECREASE

TRIGGERING INPUT WHICH INITIATES VOLTAGE SEQUENCE FROM ENVELOPE GENERATOR

VOLTS

TIME

ATTACK

INITIAL DECAY

SUSTAIN

FINAL DECAY

Basic controls and voltage output pattern of an Envelope Generator.

FIGURE 25

D. The Oscillator as a Source of Voltage Control

Although the primary function of an oscillator is to generate a signal, this signal, being a voltage, can also be used as a voltage-control source. Usually, we set the frequency of this oscillator to a very low, sub-audible range, say, 7 Hz. When we take the sine wave output and use it as a control voltage (control voltage input) of another oscillator which is producing an audio signal, the pitch of this oscillator will now vary up and down seven times a second, in effect, a *pitch vibrato*. Suppose that we take an audio signal and pass it through a voltage-controlled filter. As a control voltage on the filter, let us take our control oscillator output at 7 Hz. We will now hear a steady pitch, but the harmonics heard will vary at a rate of seven times per second as the band of frequencies passing through the filter varies in step with the control-voltage input. This can be called a *timbre vibrato*.

Suppose we pass our audio signal through a voltage-controlled amplifier. Using our control oscillator at 7 Hz. as the control-voltage source, the note will now vary in amplitude at a rate of seven times per second. This is called an *amplitude vibrato*.

If we should now use a square wave instead of a sine wave connected to the voltage-controlled amplifier (VCA), the amplifier would alternately be turned on, then off, giving us a strum effect. There are many applications in which an oscillator may be used, not just for generating a signal, but as a means of controlling voltage (Figure 26).

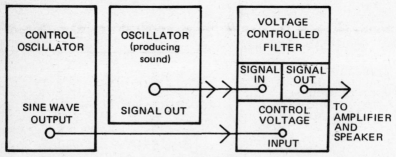

An oscillator can be used as a voltage control source to modulate a filter, amplifier or another voltage controlled oscillator.

FIGURE 26

E. The Linear Controller

Some synthesizers are supplied with a voltage-control source which consists of a metal strip stretched over a wooden base. A conductive element is built under the metal strip, and as the strip is depressed by the finger, electrical contact is made. As the finger is moved to the right, the *linear controller* produces a higher control voltage. Often, a triggering switch in the form of two additional metal bands is provided which, when touched simultaneously with the finger, will trigger an attack.

F. The Foot Pedal

A *foot pedal* may be used to provide a varying control current. As the pedal is depressed, an increasing control voltage is supplied to whichever voltage control module you wish to control.

G. The Voltage Sequencer

A unique device has been developed for supplying a series of control voltages which can be pre-set and run in a time sequence. It is called a *sequencer.*

As you recall in our discussion of pulse wave shapes, we said that square, or pulse, waves can be used as on-off switches. The basic timer on a sequencer is a voltage-controlled oscillator with a pulse wave output. It has timing controls like other voltage-controlled oscillators (VCO's), an octave or range switch, as well as a vernier fine control. It often has an output connection, which can be used like a conventional oscillator output, and a control voltage input, which can be used to regulate its speed (frequency).

A second section of the sequencer consits of a number of potentiometers (like volume control knobs) which supply voltage to an output connection. There may be 4, 8 or 12 positions to each row. There may also be one or more separate rows with their own output. There is usually a pushbutton switch to activate the position, and often there is an indicator light which shows which position is functioning, since each position works alone. Each potentiometer can raise the frequency of the oscillator it is controlling by many octaves.

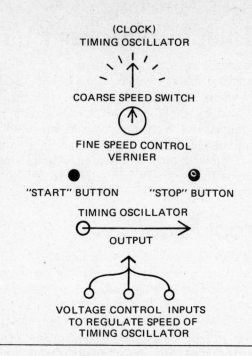

(CLOCK)
TIMING OSCILLATOR

COARSE SPEED SWITCH

FINE SPEED CONTROL
VERNIER

"START" BUTTON   "STOP" BUTTON

TIMING OSCILLATOR

OUTPUT

VOLTAGE CONTROL INPUTS
TO REGULATE SPEED OF
TIMING OSCILLATOR

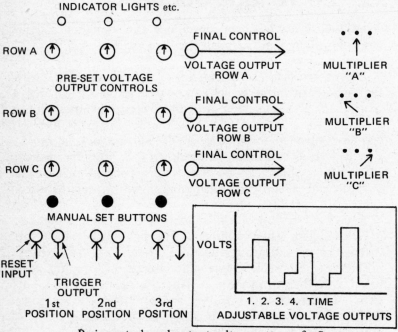

INDICATOR LIGHTS etc.

ROW A

PRE-SET VOLTAGE
OUTPUT CONTROLS

FINAL CONTROL

VOLTAGE OUTPUT
ROW A

MULTIPLIER
"A"

ROW B

FINAL CONTROL

VOLTAGE OUTPUT
ROW B

MULTIPLIER
"B"

ROW C

FINAL CONTROL

VOLTAGE OUTPUT
ROW C

MULTIPLIER
"C"

MANUAL SET BUTTONS

RESET
INPUT

TRIGGER
OUTPUT

1st
POSITION

2nd
POSITION

3rd
POSITION

VOLTS

1. 2. 3. 4.   TIME

ADJUSTABLE VOLTAGE OUTPUTS

Basic controls and output voltage pattern of a Sequencer.

FIGURE 27

Therefore, a series of pre-tuned and pre-set tones can be programmed by using the sequencer output to control an oscillator.

The pulse wave shape output of an oscillator may be used to switch something on and off. When an oscillator is used for this purpose, it is called a *clocking oscillator*. By activating the clocking oscillator with its "start" button, the pulse wave from this oscillator will switch from one sequencer position to the next to give a succession of control voltages which will cause an oscillator (VCO) to generate the frequencies comparable to the voltages pre-set on the potentiometers. The speed set for the clocking oscillator will determine how fast the oscillator frequency will change. There is usually a provision for a "repeat" so that the sequence, upon finishing the last position, will automatically recycle to the first. There is also a "disable" function switch on each position, so that it will skip whatever positions you might not want.

Each position is also provided with a triggering switch closure so that with an envelope generator and amplifier (VCA), a separate attack can be programmed for each position on the sequencer. This can also be set up by using the clocking oscillator output to close a switch and trigger the envelope generator.

If one of the rows of voltage output positions is connected back to the clocking oscillator as a control voltage, the speed of this oscillator will vary from position to position. In this way rhythmic patterns can be set up so that one position may last longer than the next.

The control voltage output of each row is independent. One row may be used for pitch control, while the second could be used simultaneously to control a filter, thus changing the timbre of each note. The sequencer is an exceptionally versatile part of the synthesizer. Although quite complex, it is basically a device using a clock to regulate the speed at which a pre-set number of control voltages will appear at its output. Sometimes voltage miltipliers are provided to double the output voltages and provide a wider swing of controls. It is worth the time it takes to learn how to use this important element of the synthesizer, particularly because of its unique effects, which are not attainable on any other instrument (Figure 27).

Summary

A number of sources of control voltages are available to us on a synthesizer: (1) a keyboard controller, consisting of a series of key switches, giving us a graduated series of voltages as well as triggering an envelope generator; (2) the envelope generator, which gives us timed ascending, sustaining and descending voltages which we can pre-set; (3) an oscillator whose wave shape and speed act as a periodic control voltage; (4) a linear controller, which is a finger-pressure device to give us variable control voltages and triggering; (5) a foot pedal for control voltage; and (6) the voltage sequencer which provides us with a timed, stepped sequence of control voltages and triggering.

These control voltage sources are very important, because their output voltage can be used to control the pitch of an oscillator (VCO), the timbre of a filter (VCF) or the loudness of each note through a voltage-controlled amplifier (VCA). Both manual and automated control voltages using these devices are available, either separately or in combination with each other. A number of other voltage-control devices can be used, ranging from a simple potentiometer to a relatively complex "joy stick" or "touch plate" system. All are devices for varying control voltages.

8. Additional Synthesizer Accessories

A number of other special devices are available which are neither voltage-controlled nor control voltage generating, but which are nevertheless useful and necessary to synthesizer programming.

A. Mixers

Mixers provide a means of combining a series of audio signals or a series of control voltages. All mixers have a series of inputs and outputs. Suppose that we were using the sound generated from three separate oscillators (VCO's), and we wanted to combine the three sounds into one combined signal. We would connect the three VCO's, each to its own input of a mixer. The mixer has its own volume control, both on each individual input, as well as on the mixed output, so we could add as little or as much of each oscillator to the final output as we wished. We can also control the final output level.

We could use the same mixer to combine a number of DC control voltages in the same way. On many mixers there are two separate outputs with a 180-degree *phase inversion*. This means that as one output may be going positive, its *complementary output* (180-degree phase shift) would be going proportionately negative. This is very useful for inverting control voltages. For example, a control voltage from an envelope generator could be used to control the pitch of an oscillator, thus making it rise two octaves. The inversion of this control voltage could be used simultaneously to make another oscillator descend two octaves.

B. Mults (Multables)

Mults are simply a number of connectors wired together. If you have a single control voltage and you want to distribute it to two or three other modules, you use a mult to get enough connections from a single source. An electrical AC wall outlet is an example of a mult. The same current is available from either outlet. They are simply sockets wired together.

C. Attenuators

Attenuators are separate potentiometers mounted with an input connection and an output connection. They are a convenience, for situations in which a signal or control voltage has to be reduced in amplitude. An attenuator is a simple "volume control."

D. Envelope Followers

Envelope followers are usually used in conjunction with external signal sources. They are provided with a signal input, although they do not treat the signal in any way, and an alternate course must be provided for the signal through other treating sections of the synthesizer. The envelope follower measures the level of the signal that it receives and, at a settable point, will trigger an envelope generator. A common use for this is to *filter sweep* an external source. This means to vary the frequencies that can pass through the filter. For example, if you wanted to filter sweep a bass drum, you would pick up the bass drum through a microphone, amplify the signal, mult the signal so that part would go to a filter and part would go to an envelope follower, which in turn, would trigger an envelope generator whose voltage control output would go to a control input on a voltage-controlled filter, thus sweeping the filter in a pre-set pattern every time the bass drum was struck.

The envelope follower is a level-sensing device. Upon receiving a signal of sufficient strength, it acts to trigger (start) an envelope generator. The voltage-controlling output of the envelope generator can then be used to control a VCO, VCF or VCA. The envelope follower is sometimes called a *Schmitt trigger*.

E. Reverberation Units

Reverberation units are used to create an artificial reverberation effect. It consists of a coil spring driven at one end by a magnet and wire coil (like a loudspeaker), with a type of microphone at the other end. The input signal drives the spring into vibration and the resonant characteristics of the spring are added to the input sound, together with the time delay that it takes for the sound to travel down the spring. There is usually a control knob which mixes the input signal with the reverberation signal in varying degrees to create a number of interesting effects at its output.

In the recording studio, reverberation is often obtained in a similar fashion. A loudspeaker driver (permanent magnet with moving coil) is attached to a suspended steel plate. A number of microphones (pick-ups) are placed along the edge of the steel sheet. The sound vibrations are transmitted through the steel sheet, with varying time delays to the various microphones.

F. Ring Modulators

A ring modulator is a device for causing two separate signals to interact with each other. One input is called the *carrier* while the second input is called the *signal*.

If we were to feed a sine wave signal of 500 Hz. into the ring modulator together with a carrier signal of 600 Hz., we would get the algebraic sum of the two signals: 100 Hz. (600 Hz. minus 500 Hz.) and 1,100 Hz. (600 Hz. plus 500 Hz.). In a true ring modulator, both the original signal and the carrier are suppressed at the output.

The resultant *clangerous* sound (similar to a large struck bell) is extremely useful. If the signal pitch is changed and the carrier signal remains at a fixed pitch, each different sound will have a different timbre. If both signal and carrier change in step, the same timbre will be maintained on each separate pitch played.

A good ring modulator is a very useful device in the creation of electronic music. A similar effect can be achieved, however, by *frequency modulation.* If you refer back to "Voltage Control Sources" in Chapter 7, we used an oscillator as a control voltage source to control the pitch of another oscillator. If we increase the speed of this controlling oscillator to an audio frequency, we will get an effect similar to a ring modulator. We could also get an interesting effect similar to ring modulation by *amplitude modulation.* If the output of our controlling oscillator were fed into a voltage-controlled amplifier (control voltage input), an interesting effect could be achieved as a signal from a signal oscillator, passing through the VCA, would be turned on and off at an audio frequency.

Summary

A series of accessories are provided on the synthesizer which are neither signal-generating nor control-voltage-generating devices. These are used for mixing, inverting, multing, triggering and adding artificial reverberation.

Ring modulation is the interaction of two audio signals which produce an output consisting of the algebraic sum of the two signals. Frequency modulation and amplitude modulation can produce a somewhat similar effect.

9. Interconnecting Various Synthesizer Components

A. Introduction

The incredible number of tonal resources possible in the synthesizer are partially due to the fact that the various sections of the synthesizer can be interconnected in almost endless ways. We have found that we have three basic circuits with which to be concerned: (1) the signal circuit, which must be complete from signal source (oscillator, white-pink noise generator and external sound source) to final amplifier and speaker; (2) control voltage circuits (keyboard, sequencer, linear controller, envelope generator, foot pedal, etc.) which must be connected to various control voltage inputs on oscillators, filters and amplifiers; and (3) triggering devices (keyboard, sequencer, etc.) which must be connected to envelope generators in order to activate them.

B. Patch Cord Connectors

Patch cord connectors consist of pieces of wire with standard "banana" or "phone" plugs on either end. To route a signal, control voltage, or trigger, these male plugs are inserted into the appropriate *jacks* (female connections) from one section to another. The procedure is identical to that of the familiar telephone switchboard. Patch cords come in various lengths and are usually color coded as to length so that they can easily be traced. Normally, signals should go to signal jacks, control voltages should go to control voltage jacks and triggers should go to triggering jacks. On some units, a special two-pronged plug is used exclusively for triggering circuits. As usual, an "output" jack from one unit can be connected by means of a patch cord to the "input" jack of another unit.

C. Switching

Various types of switches may be used to interconnect the

various components of the synthesizer. Some are regular on-off switches which add a section to the circuit. Then there is the more complex selector switch with multiple positions. These multi-position switches are used in conjunction with common line or wires, which we call *buss bars*. Suppose we wanted to take a signal output from an oscillator and connect it to the input of a filter. The oscillator is internally connected to the selector switch which can be used to put the signal on any one of an assortment of buss bars. Once the signal has been assigned to a buss bar (or just "buss"), it can then be taken off the buss through a selector switch, which is internally connected to the input of the filter, thus completing the circuit from oscillator to filter.

D. Pin Matrixing

Pin matrixing is a method of interconnecting various components of the system by means of metal pins which are inserted into holes in a panel, making electrical contacts in accordance with what has been pre-wired underneath the panel. A number of components are listed along the top edge of the matrix and another set of components is listed along one side. If a metal pin is inserted at the point of intersection, an electrical contact is established between them.

E. Multi-System Switching

On most synthesizers a combination of switching systems may be used. With a patch cord system the most common connections, such as keyboard control voltage to an oscillator, are made with switches. However, the bulk of the system is patch cord. On multi-position switch systems, alternate means of patch cording are often provided for special applications, although the primary connections are made through switches.

Regardless of the interconnecting system, keep in mind that there are three main circuits which must be completed for the synthesizer to work: (1) the *signal* circuit, consisting of an oscillator, white-pink noise generator or external sound source; (2) a *control voltage* circuit and (3) a *triggering* circuit.

An electrical path must be provided from the sound (signal) source, through whatever sound modifiers you wish to use (filters, etc.), through the voltage-controlled amplifier, and eventually out to the main amplifier and speaker system, so that the sound may be heard in the studio. From the sound source the path could go directly to the voltage-controlled amplifier, then back through the sound-modifying elements in any order that you wish to set up, but eventually there has to be a complete electrical path from sound source to sound reproducer (amplifier and speaker). Provision is usually made by means of a final mixer so that not only the monitor amplifier and speaker in the studio are given the final signal, but also a tape recorder may be fed the signal so that you can record simultaneously.

A control voltage path must be provided from the control voltage generators (keyboard, foot pedal, oscillator, envelope generator, etc.) to whatever sound-modifying and -controlling sections you wish to control.

A triggering path must be provided from a triggering source (keyboard, sequencer, etc.) to the envelope generators. Sometimes you might want to mult (split) this triggering to control two or more envelope generators. You might want to use one envelope generator to control amplitude (through a VCA), a second envelope generator to change the filter characteristics as the tone is in progress, and a third envelope generator to control a voltage-controlled oscillator (VCO) to make a timed change of pitch.

Summary

The flexibility of sound generation on the synthesizer is possible due to the various sound-generating, -treating and -amplifying functions which can be interconnected and controlled in a great number of different ways. In order to interconnect, a system of patch cords and jacks, switches or pin matrixing may be used, either alone or in combination. A complete path must be provided for the three circuits of the synthesizer, the signal, control voltages and triggers.

10. Salient Features of Various Synthesizers

Today, numerous manufacturers supply synthesisers for the amateur and professional alike. Some, like the ARP Pro Soloist, are specifically designed for easy-use applications. Others, such as the Putney AKS, require a higher degree of skill on the part of the player. Then there is another caregory of synthesisers, those with preset controls that restrict the output signal to recognisable musical tones, most usually those of stringed instruments.

Synthesiser technology is developing at a fast rate, and new models are always being put on the market. So any specific information on current models is likely to soon go out of date. However, it is useful to see how the theories that we have learned are put into practical performance by briefly looking at the specifications of four available synthesisers:

A. ARP Pro-Soloist

Thirty preset instrumental and electronic effects are instantly available via a keyboard that is as convenient to operate as an electronic organ. The touch-sensitive keyboard allows the player to increase the volume of brilliance, add vibrator on "wow", bend the note or make it "growl." Among the main controls are the portmento, which enables the pitch to slide from note to note, and the associated portmento speed, which regulates the time required for the slide effect. Further controls include volume, repeat, repeat/vibrato speed and octave transpose switch. The preset instrument effects range from flute and tuba to steel drum and fuzz guitar.

B. ARP Odyssey

A remarkably flexible instrument, the Odyssey was designed for use by discriminating musicians for both live use and for studio work. In addition to the capabilities of the Pro-Soloist, the Odyssey has a two-voice polyphonic keyboard with a white/pink noise generator, plus a sample-and-hold function which enables the player to create series of random pitches and improvisational effects. A digital ring modulator creates extremely complex tone colours through controlled distortion. An audio mixer allows the mixing of outputs from the two voltage-controlled oscillators, and the noise generator or ring modulator. The voltage – controlled filter permits the control of tone colour, or timbre, to an exact degree. The high-pass filter add an extra brilliance. The envelope generator enables you to control the attack, decay, sustain and release time of each note. There are three oscillators – one with pulse-width modulated output, one with a phase-locked synchronisation feature and pulse-width modulated output, and the third with a low frequency output.

C. EMS Synthi–AKS

Fitted into a briefcase-sized container, the AKS has a tremendously flexible range of capabilities. Through compact digital sequencing circuitary, repeatable ssequences of up to 256 notes can be stored. The synthsiser is operated via a touch-sensitive keyboard. A pin matrix system is used to link the various oscillators and control devices into an almost infinite number of combinations. The AKS can be used – in conjunction with tape machines and mixers – to play electronic music of the most complex and adventurous kind.

The AKS has three oscillators, a variable noise generator, a multi-purpose filter/oscillator, a ring modulator, a sophisitcated envelope shaper, a reverberation unit and the capability of being used with various EMS ancillary units.

Conclusion

In this book we have attempted to explain the nature of sound and how it is used to create music—especially electronically. We have emphasized the necessity of a basic knowledge of acoustics and the fundamentals of electricity in order to work not only in electronic music but in any field of contemporary music today. Music is now a product of tapes and records, as well as live concert performance, and a knowledge of the tape recorder, recording techniques and reproduction equipment has therefore become as essential to the musician as a knowledge of theory and harmony.

We have explained the broad general principles of the electronic generation of music rather than to teach certain set procedures by rote. We feel that if you understand each function of each piece of equipment, new and creative ideas are more likely to result. Rather than describe specific interconnections, to produce, say, a flute sound, it is much more important to be able to analyze a flute sound and then produce it from a knowledge of how to combine the elements by means of the synthesizer.

This text is intended for use in conjunction with actual electronic music equipment, since, as with any musical instrument, without touch and practice, it becomes an intellectual exercise, with little real meaning.

It is the author's hope that a new generation of musicians will grow up with the synthesizer as a standard music-making instrument, that their knowledge of the instrument will be first-hand and not merely a carryover from more conventional instruments. In this way new music will surely evolve, using the language of the synthesizer as a means of human expression and communication.